Tropic of Cancer

TAMAULIPAS

Sierra Madre Oriental

Tampico

TARO

HIDALGO

XICO

D.F.

Cuernavaca

MORELOS

TLAXCALA

Puebla Amozoc

PUEBLA

Huaquechula

Izucar de Matamoros

Acatlan

Olinala

VERACRUZ

Veracruz

GULF OF MEXICO

OAXACA

Atzompa

Oaxaca Teotitlan del Valle

San Bartolo de Coyotepec

Tlacolula

To Yucatan Peninsula

Sierra Madre del Sur

GULF OF TEHUANTEPEC

UNITE

GULF OF MEXICO

Saltillo

Tropic of Cancer

CUBA

MEXICO

YUCATAN
PENINSULA

PACIFIC OCEAN

CENTRAL AMERICA

Large map shows Central Mexico from the lower tip
of the Yucatan Peninsula up to the Tropic of Cancer.

D1062619

CRAFTS
OF
MEXICO

CRAFTS
OF
MEXICO

Marian
Harvey

PHOTOGRAPHS BY
Ken Harvey

Macmillan Publishing Co., Inc.
NEW YORK

Collier Macmillan Publishers
LONDON

To Ken

Macmillan Publishing Co., Inc.
Collier-Macmillan Canada Ltd.

Library of Congress Catalog Card Number: 72-86037

FIRST PRINTING 1973

Printed in the United States of America

CONTENTS

v

PART III
Metals

PART IV
Clay

PART V
Wood

PART VI
Paper

CONTENTS

vi

ACKNOWLEDGMENTS

All the craftsmen we visited were helped by someone at some time; that is why they are in their craft today. I was helped, too.

First, I thank my husband, Ken Harvey, for taking the photographs. I thank both him and our daughter, Hiliry, for traveling with me the 3,000 miles within Mexico to visit the crafts. I thank Mindy Hoschler, our older daughter, who took care of affairs at home during our long absence.

I wish to thank Elizabeth Cuellar, Mexican folk art expert and writer, who traveled with us and upon whose knowledge I often depended.

Particular thanks I give to Leonard Brooks, artist and writer, who suggested that I write this book and guided me during its initial planning.

To Reva Brooks and Tom Myers, photographers, who gave valuable photographic assistance and advice.

To my mother, Marian D. Myers, an editor; to my father, the late Thomas F. Myers, Jr., a publisher; to Earle Birney, Canadian poet and his wife, Esther; and to the late Ashmead Scott, screenwriter, for helping me when I first began to write.

To Tom Scott and Robert Somerlott of the Instituto Allende Writing Center.

To Guillermo Gaete who executed the drawings.

To the people who gave help and technical advice on the particular crafts: John Paddock, anthropologist of Oaxaca, for great aid in unraveling the mysteries of the black pottery of Coyotepec; to Albert Levy, ceramics; Kent Bowman, silver; and Bill Brewer, weaving. To all of San Miguel, whose knowledge of the intricacies of their particular craft they generously shared. To Felix Perez Juarez for the history of San Miguel weaving. To Joan Robertson for technical help in mixing the wax for the *nearika.*

To Jeanne and Guy Schlee for help in many of the crafts besides their own. To Sterling Dickinson and Judy Martin for general information. To Carmen Buenrostro who remembered San Miguel of thirty years ago, and to José Flores who made the frames, stripped the reeds, etc., so I could try the crafts.

To Licenciado Primo C. Martinez Tamayo, Jefe del Departamento de Artesanías of the Banco Fomento.

To Juanita Peñaloza, our friend of many years, who first introduced us to the crafts of Mexico.

To Connie Schrader of the The Macmillan Company. To Susan Shipman, recently of Macmillan.

To the people aboard the Italian freighter, the *M/N Antonio Pacinotti,* where I typed the final draft of the manuscript and, in particular, to Aldo Cotti of Genoa, who fixed my typewriter when we were on the middle of the ocean.

Last—to all the craftsmen.

ACKNOWLEDGMENTS

INTRODUCTION

Mexico's tradition of *artesanía* goes back for centuries. Many crafts have endured to this day, sometimes within the same families, who for generations have passed down their techniques. But, in the last twenty years particularly, there has been change. Some of the traditional crafts have almost disappeared; others have become mechanized.

When Cortés sent samples of Mexican crafts to Europe, Dürer is reported to have said, ". . . And as for myself, I have never in all the days of my life seen things that so delighted my heart. For I saw among them wonderful works of art and was astonished at the subtle ingenuity of the men of those distant lands. . . ."

The visitor to Mexico today, some 450 years later, is astonished still. In all the Americas, Mexico maintains the richest and most varied production of the crafts. It rates as one of the greatest producers of handcrafts in the world.

Yet, the craftsmen of Mexico enjoys no particular distinction among his countrymen. He is anonymous. Few sign their works. This is historical, for to be a craftsman in Mexico is not in any way unusual.

Today, 60 percent of the people have crowded into the cities—mainly into Mexico City where the pay is the highest in the country. Here, the greater metropolitan population has swelled to some 8 million. Twenty years ago it was 3 million.

Mexico has come a long way since the troubled days of its many revolutions, days which persisted until fifty years ago. Today her gross national product is fifteenth in the world. It is not surprising then, that while striving to become an industrial nation, Mexico has turned its main interest from the poor countryman, the *campesino*, to the production of manufactured goods. Yet the *campesino* has not been completely forsaken. One of Mexico's greatest incomes still comes from the tourist industry, and most of the tourists still come from the United States. These tourists come not because Mexico builds Fords or washing machines, but because she retains some of her "primitive" charm.

Luis Echeverriá, the new President, has declared and so far carried out the proposition that the long-neglected Indian will be aided. When we left Mexico, he had already spent the first eighty days of his single, six-year tenure at work—no days off. Each weekend he went to different parts of the country to see firsthand what the people needed. By the following Monday, work had already begun.

Among the 5 million who moved to Mexico City in the last twenty years has been the craftsman. He moved to the city hoping he would find a better life. If he was a basket weaver, he couldn't bring his *carrizo* with him. The ceramist left his clay behind. Some continue valiantly. Others have given in to quicker and easier ways to make their craft—such as many of the lacquer workers have done.

All have to sell to live. They must make what the customer wants. In the areas where there has been a great rise in the middle class, the crafts have suffered. The new midde class Mexican has notoriously bad taste. He wants—or rather his wife wants—frilly, white "porcelain" dishes decorated with little pink roses. Judging from the markets around Guadalajara and Guanajuato, he has also been known to buy tiny, flowered ceramic toilets which he uses as objets d'art. The poor Mexican, however, continues to use his natural wool blanket of the old design; he still eats from earthenware bowls made the same way they were centuries ago.

Mexico has received a rich heritage from its ancient civilizations. Though I refer a great deal to the Aztec civilization, it had only been in power some 300 years before the Conquest. Many civilizations existed before, and many different groups lived at the same time as the Aztecs. The Aztecs receive most frequent attention, because they were there when the Spanish came. They were in their ascendency, and these are the people who were written about from firsthand experience.

Everyday the newspapers report new archaeological findings. While we were there, 200 sculptures were found in a circular grave in Michoacán. Even the circular grave, itself, was a new find—one had never been found in Mexico before. When Mexico City was building its beautiful Metro, work was stopped constantly because of archaeological discoveries which had to be carefully photographed, extricated, and catalogued.

The Indian often knows little of his past. He knows as little—and often less—than others do about the history, the chemical, and even the physical properties of his materials. This seems particularly true of the traditional ceramist. He knows that he must use a certain earth, that he must fire his clay so long. He thinks he must use a certain material for his fire, but he does not always know why it works, and his reasons for its working often have nothing to do with the real reasons. But, the point is, he does use the right material to achieve the result he wants. And he has used whatever he has found near at hand to achieve it. Being poor, he is ingenious.

This situation is certainly not true of some of Mexico's new artists such as Jorge Wilmot of Tonalá. This ceramist uses a fine degree of technical knowledge to produce a highly fired, strong pottery. Unique in itself, this pottery is completely Mexican. Wilmot, who is known throughout the world, is the winner of several international awards.

The traditional Indian craftsman will remember that his parents, his grandparents, and perhaps even his great grandparents were involved in his craft. Before that he knows little, but he is not so different from his North American contemporary. How many of us can trace our families back a 1000 years—or even 500?

Of course, the Mexican's life has not been so fluid as ours, but certainly the Conquest, and later the revolutions upset his life. Families moved, work stopped. Those craftsmen who remembered the Revolution of 1910, spoke of great chaos.

Most Mexicans today are mestizo: the literal term meaning a person who is a mixture of the Indian and the Spanish. The term, Indian, is supposed to mean a person who is solely of Indian lineage. *Campesino* is supposed to mean a farmer. But these are not the real translations. Today, Indian means *campesino* as well. Whether he is mestizo or not, if he lives in the old way, if he sleeps on a *petate*, cooks on a charcoal burner, eats tortillas and beans, he is Indian. If he lives in the country (and sometimes the city), his house has a dirt floor. He dislikes light —it is not good for him. The only light is usually from one door, perhaps one window. He has no running water. He dresses in the traditional ways. (Though "traditional" today in some parts of the country may mean Levis for the men, the women always wear a *rebozo*, a shawl.) He is not educated. He has retained his old way of life, his old way of thinking. He is caught. Generally, he will continue the crafts because he knows nothing else.

Mestizo has come to mean a Mexican, no matter what lineage, who lives in the European way. He cooks on a stove, eats at a table, and sleeps on a bed. He has running water. He is educated.

As more and more children of the craftsmen are educated, it appears that fewer will go into the crafts. Several of the mestizo craft families we met spoke of this. It was not only that the children often didn't want to follow in their parents' footsteps, but that the craftsmen themselves felt it was a difficult way to make a living. If their children were educated, they wanted them to go into something "better." Whether they went into teaching, perhaps a goverment job, into the church, or another field—it would be worth a try.

For the Indian craftsman there was little question that he would continue. Indian children had worked in the craft from the time they were seven or eight. They would continue, probably, for the rest of their lives. They have little choice.

Many of the craftsmen we visited were actually innovators in their fields. They had taken an old product and done something new with it, such as Plácido Pablo of the *corazón de trigo* (Chapter 6), Doña Rosa of the black pottery (Chapter 10), and Teodora Blanco of the "sculptured" clay (Chapter 11). Although one could say they were outside the mainstream of modern Mexican life, they have nevertheless become well-known and respected in international craft fields. Except for Doña Rosa, they live poorly; they live like their neighbors. Perhaps the only visible difference is that they have a few more small, one-door buildings in their dirt-surfaced compounds and that they dress a little better, though still in the traditional way. If you were to pass any of these craftsmen on the street, you would not know they were renowned in their fields.

These are the "Indian" craftsmen. Others live quite well. Certainly we saw the most humble as well as one of the most beautiful houses of Mexico. The last belonged to a "new" craftsman—a European.

In our visits to the craftsmen we were never refused hospitality. We were always offered a chair, the fruit from a tree—in a sense, whatever they had. No matter how poor they were, we were always given a gift—much to our embarrassment—when we left. They gave freely of their time and their knowledge. They knew they were good craftsmen, but I don't think they knew, really, how good. Their sphere went little beyond their daily life, perhaps a few trips to Mexico City.

The craftsman makes very little for the long hours he works and he does not receive enough profit from his product. Often the craftsman himself doesn't consider his time as an economic factor. He often charges little more than the cost of his materials. But by the time these crafts reach the stores, the price is twice as high or more. This means that someone else is receiving the bulk of the profit. The middlemen make the money. This was true thirty years ago according to books written during that time and it is true today.

The craftsman knows this. But along with the rest of his countrymen, he is a cynic. Little is put over on him. He knows exactly what is going on. That is the way it has always been; that is the way it will always be. He accepts it.

I have tried to check all my sources—both verbal and written. Early in my research, I discovered that what was written was not always so, but had been researched from previous books that were mistaken in the first place. Also, in the light of new archaelogical findings— emerging every day—it was necessary to discount some of what I read, anyway. For these reasons, I checked my facts with an authority in every case. If I could not verify them, then I have indicated this in the text. I did not at any time go by hearsay except, of course, when the craftsmen themselves recounted their personal histories. Sometimes it took hours to watch a single object being made. Afterwhile, the people began to talk, to reminisce, to tell about their lives, what they thought about life, their work. Much of the information in this book has never been written before.

When general technical information seemed necessary in the how-to-do-it sections, I have suggested certain basic books the reader can use. Any good book will do.

My approaches to the various crafts differ. In some cases a general background of particular information was needed to explain a process that was repeated many times, such as in weaving the serape, the *petate*, and in lacquering. For other items such as the *santo* and the fish of silver, a step-by-step approach was best.

Once in the center of Mexico, we traveled 3,000 miles to visit the crafts. But those I chose are more or less centered in five central regions of Mexico. They are (1) the State of Mexico and Puebla, (2) the Bajío—the high central plateau of Mexico, (3) Guadalajara, (4) Oaxaca, and (5) Pátzcuaro.

Included in this book are the addresses of the craftsmen visited (see pages 239-241). The reader could use these as a guide if he were to travel part or all of this route.

It would be helpful to know Spanish, in most cases, necessary unless someone with you knows the language. For some reason, the craftsman will receive you more freely if only foreigners are present. He knows most of his countrymen are not that interested in his work, so if a Mexican is present, he must be there for another reason. That guide you bring may be a tax collector, a government official, or someone who will bring him trouble. Remember, many of these craftsmen cannot read or write and they have a great fear of anything or anybody that might look official. They know the tourist is not.

The reader should also know he will have to patiently seek some of these craftsmen for some of their neighbors don't seem to know who they are. Even though the craftsman is well-known in his field, you may also find that he will want to be paid to have you watch him make his product. This is in addition to buying the craft, or its equivalent, when he is finished. It is the Indian craftsman who does this, not the mestizo. But he is poor and you cannot blame him.

We worked out from a central spot: San Miguel de Allende. It could be Mexico City or another town. We covered the areas in three different trips, each taking about two weeks. (This did not include the time taken for the crafts in San Miguel itself—another two to three weeks.)

Besides visiting the craftsmen described here, we visited many others while gathering general information. Particularly rich in crafts is the Oaxaca region where for ten days we visited craftsmen. We saw many weavers. We watched backstrap weavers, candle makers, silver workers, others. Pátzcuaro, too, is noted for its many crafts. But so are all the regions.

In each of the five general regions I chose, there are many more crafts than those covered in this book. This is true, also, for the rest of the country. I chose these particular crafts for a number of reasons. First, to include some crafts from each of the six general fields: weaving, reeds, wood, clay, paper, and metals. I had to limit myself to an itinerary that was physically possible to cover. In other words I wanted to group the crafts geographically as well. I wanted to choose some crafts that are well known and some relatively unknown, some that are pre-Conquest and some that are post-Conquest, the colonial and the "new." I wanted some "Indian" crafts and some mestizo crafts. I wanted a cross section, all possible ways.

I hope the reader will enjoy this venture into the crafts of Mexico as much as I have.

INTRODUCTION

WEAVING

OJO DE DIOS 1

A Huichol Indian drives the central shaft of an *ojo de dios* into the dirt floor of his hut. It is a stick cross containing only the central woven eye.

His wife has just given birth to another child. For each of the first five years of this child's life, he will add another eye. When the child becomes five, the *ojo* will be complete (Plate 1).

Eighty percent of the children in this untamed, mountainous region of Jalisco and Nayarit do not live to their fifth year. For additional protection, the Huichol thrusts a prayer arrow into the *ojo*'s side (Figure 1).

The *ojo de dios* is used to secure health and long life for children. It is the wand—the eye—through which the eye of god will see the supplicant. Implanted in sacred caves, it is also a symbol through which the gods are worshipped. The prayer arrow permits the Huichol to enter into direct contact with his gods. It is a magic instrument of petition.

With luck, the *ojo* will "grow" until it stands, several sticks bound at right angles, brightly woven diamonds set at each successive end with four small diamonds encircling the central eye, the center of the universe.

FIGURE 1

The Huicholes live on the pinnacles of Mexico's inaccessible west central Sierra Madre mountains. Still a semi-autonomous group, they are divided into five "ranchos"—not villages—and cling to a style of life that was ancient when the Spanish came. Though they numbered 20,000 at the beginning of the twentieth century, only 8,000 remain in the region.

They are little influenced by the world beyond their mountains, although this may change in a few years when new roads are built. For now, the Huicholes still feel that all things are either "authentic," or Spanish. Authentic means Huichol; everything else is Spanish, or foreign.

The Huicholes worship gods of earth, air, fire, water, and many others. Curiously, there is no one word for god in the Huichol language; they use Grandmother, Grandfather, Great Grandfather, or even

Our Mother Eagle Girl. The cross of the *ojo de dios* is that of the legendary four directions: earth, fire, water, and air. It is not in any way the cross of Christ. Their art is directed to the gods of nature.

They are, however, influenced by Christianity. In the early 1700's, Franciscan friars built their first missions in this harsh country. Now, Padre Ernesto de Loera Ochoa heads the mission at Zapopan, Jalisco. His photographic blow-ups of Huichol life decorate the walls of the museum store there. Called Father Camera or sometimes Father Wind by the Huicholes, the padre always flies into Huichol territory because walking is the only other way and a journey on foot takes two or three weeks. Even flying in may still mean a half-day's walk to one of the missions—often straight up the rugged mountainside. We wanted to go, however, and a Huichol at the Zapopan mission offered to be our guide.

At the Zapopan mission, a few kilometers from Guadalajara, cluster some of the Huicholes who have left their mountain homeland. They travel between the two "countries," walking or occasionally flying. Jesus Valenzuela Ortiz lives in both worlds. When we met him in the churchyard of the Basilica of Zapopan, he wore a straw hat edged with red felt from which were suspended conical dried seed pods. His wide pants were embroidered with stylized animals, flowers, birds, and geometric patterns, and over his shirt he wore an embroidered cape. Around his waist, already girdled by many woven belts, hung several small bags secured by a single cord; each bag woven with designs of religious significance. The Huichol man, like the peacock, dresses much more flamboyantly than the woman who wears long skirts of embroidered homespun cotton, blouses, and a large embroidered covering called a *quechuemitl*.

It was Jesus Valenzuela who had offered to take us to his home country, Santa Catarina. He was at the mission to help make the large *ojos de dios* and the *nearikas* (Chapter 2) which are made and sold to help raise money for the mission. Some of these commercial *ojos* are complicated structures, four feet high with as many as thirty-nine diamonds on a series of crossed sticks. These were not traditional, however, for the ritual *ojo* is 15 inches tall and has only five diamonds. Antonio Pineda would teach us to make it. He is fifteen and although he remembers Rancho Santa Catarina from which he came four or five years ago, he speaks only a few words of Huichol now and wears only "Spanish"—western—clothes.

Although not authentic, many well-made *ojos* are available in

Mexico. Boys sell a new kind of *ojo* at the gas stations in Tepic, a gateway to the resort of Puerto Vallarta. These small, well-made *ojos* in marvelous colors have only a central eye which hangs on wound yarn to be worn as a necklace. In an excellent craft store near the center of Tepic, free-standing *ojos* are on sale. Some that are only 8 inches high are used as paperweights. These *ojos* are set in a cylindrical form, probably secured by plaster of paris, with bark wound around the base. Others are several feet tall, freeform *ojos* with dramatic decorations intended for use as a sculpture. These adaptations of the old art form were pleasing and well designed.

Spurious Huichol art, however, has appeared in the last few years. Poor examples can be found around Guadalarjara: *ojos* of loosely woven thin wool in lackluster colors. A town in Puebla makes *ojos*, but these are copies of the Huichol. A village in the southern state of Chiapas is said to weave them, but the *ojo de dios* is native in Mexico solely to the Huicholes. Only two other places in the world are said to weave them, Chile and Tibet.

Working with the Craftsman

TOOLS AND MATERIALS

6 reeds or dowels. You will need four reeds or dowels 3¾ inches; one, 25 inches; one, 15 inches. For the crossed sticks the Huicholes use a reed called *caral* which is lightweight, straight, and smooth, but ¼ inch diameter dowels can be substituted. These often can be bought in long lengths and cut easily. Place the blade of the knife on the dowel at the section where you wish to cut it. Then, while pressing down on the blade, roll the dowel. This simultaneous pressing and rolling will result in a nice clean cut.

2 skeins of yarn. In more than two colors if you prefer. The model in Plate 1 is blue and black, blue representing the sea, and black for north and death. Not a very happy combination, but these were the only colors available the day we were there.

While the yarn for the fringe is 3-ply, the yarn for the weaving of the eye is single-ply (1/16 inch in diameter). It would be difficult to match a single-ply and multiple-ply yarn. I suggest you use single- or very fine multiple-ply throughout. Swedish Hargarn (a source readily available although not quite as colorful as the Mexican) is a single-ply yarn slightly thicker than the yarn of the model. A very fine 4-ply Portuguese yarn is available. If possible, buy the yarn in stitchery skeins which contain about ¼ ounce of yarn. The *ojo* is made from one ounce of yarn.

PROCEDURE

1. Antonio lines up the 25-inch and the 15-inch staves so that they are parallel and align at the top. Halfway down, he wraps blue yarn around the two staves (Figure 2) and twists them at right angles to make a cross (Figure 3).

· 2. Then he winds yarn around the cross sticks four times the other way and twists them to test their tightness, for the staves must be wrapped securely.

3. Since the three upper points of the cross must be the same distance from the center, Antonio uses the yarn as a measuring device. Adjustments are made if necessary.

4. He winds the yarn around the intersection four times in each direction before starting to make the central blue diamond, the Huichol center of the universe. The process remains the same throughout: wind

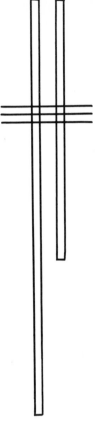

FIGURE **2**

FIGURE **3**

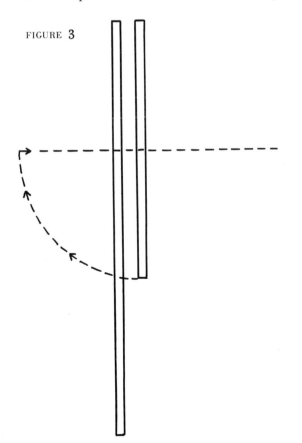

OJO DE DIOS

13

the yarn over the staff, under the same staff, then up over the next staff, under it, and so on (Figure 4). Keep the yarn taut at all times and place the strands close together. Do not overlap.

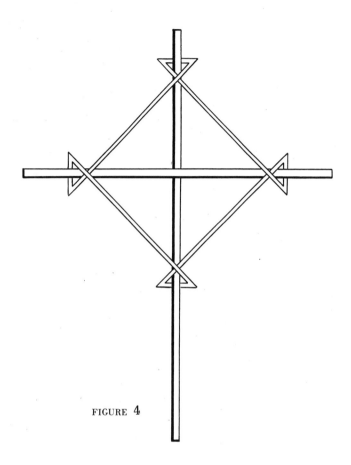

FIGURE 4

5. When the center diamond is 1½ inches deep, Antonio breaks off the blue yarn, but he does not release the yarn when reaching for the other color. All materials are kept near at hand. Before connecting the blue and the black yarn, he twists the ends so they are trim and then he makes a square knot which will not show (Figure 5).

Antonio's little sister, Teresa, had been unwinding yarn for him as he worked. Later, when she grew tired, he placed the skein around his knees and ankles.

6. Now with the black yarn, he continues to weave the central diamond in the same way as before. If you are following the design of the model (Plate 1), this band of black will be about ¼ inch wide (Figure 6). Remember to keep the yarn taut as you work.

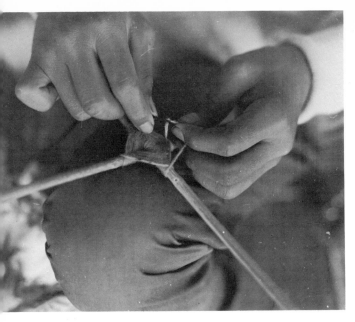
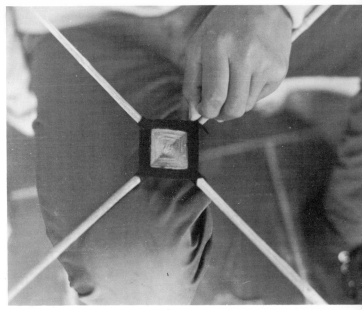

FIGURE **5**   FIGURE **6**

7. After he has woven the $\frac{1}{4}$ inch of black, Antonio ties on more blue yarn, twisting the ends first. He continues to weave around the staves in the same way until he has $\frac{1}{4}$ inch of blue.

8. Now he joins the blue to more black yarn and finishes the central diamond with another black band, $\frac{1}{4}$ inch deep. At this point he does not break off the yarn, but instead winds the yarn two inches down the central staff and knots it (Figure 7).

9. He takes a $3\frac{3}{4}$-inch staff and lines it up with the top of the central staff as was done in Figure 2.

10. Wrapping the yarn half way down around the two staves, he twists them to make a cross and repeats Steps 2 through 8. These smaller diamonds will be about half the size of the central diamond. They are sometimes woven on both sides of the staff, but this is not necessary. Antonio wove them only on one. Continue to keep the yarn taut, giving it a firm, but gentle tug every so often if it becomes slack.

11. Now Antonio winds the black yarn down around the central staff to the central diamond and knots it 2 or 3 times (Figure 8).

12. He takes the second $3\frac{3}{4}$-inch staff and lines it up with one end of the crossbar, makes a cross, and begins Steps 2 through 8 again (Figure 9). When this diamond is complete, he winds the yarn around the main crossbar back to the central diamond.

FIGURE **7**

FIGURE 8

FIGURE 9

13. With the third 3¾-inch staff, Antonio repeats the processes forming a diamond at the other end of the crossbar. When done, he winds the yarn around the staff again back to the central diamond.

14. Now, Antonio takes the fourth 3¾-inch staff. He lines it up from the bottom of the central diamond (Figure 10), not the bottom of the staff, twists it to form a cross, and weaves the last diamond. This time he winds the black yarn up to the central diamond and knots it several times.

15. With one strand of blue and one of black, he twists the yarn from the base of the lower diamond down the central staff, leaving a few inches free at the bottom. He does this by twirling the yarn on the staff.

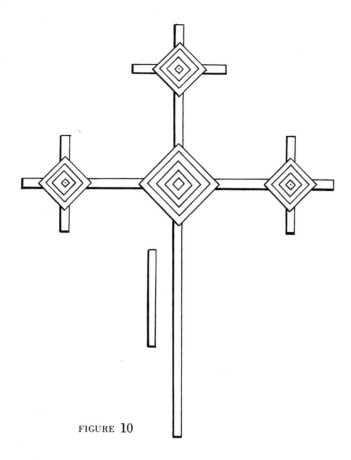

FIGURE 10

So far it has taken Antonio a half hour. The *ojo* is complete except for the tassels.

16. The tassels are made assembly-line style. Using both blue and black, Antonio puts the two strands together. (Teresa busies herself tying remnants of the blue yarn to longer lengths so there is no waste.) He doubles the two rows of yarn and then redoubles them until the length measures about 33 inches. Then he cuts every three inches giving him 11 tassels. (If the fringe is cut any shorter, you will have trouble binding it.) He repeats the process so he will have 22 tassels. You will need only 11 tassels altogether as there are 11 exposed ends on the *ojo*, but they are doubled later so cut 22. Each half tassel contains about 14 strands, but there can be more.

17. Antonio sets out the 22 tassels on the church patio in neat well-spaced rows (Figure 11) and binds each successive tassel onto each exposed end of the *ojo*, from the bottom right, clockwise, continuing on

OJO DE DIOS

17

FIGURE 11

FIGURE 12

around the *ojo* (Figure 12). He places the *ojo* over one half tassel on the patio floor and sets another half tassel directly on top of the exposed end. 1½ inches of the tassel are free; the other 1½ inches goes up over the staff. Now holding half a tassel beneath the staff end and the other half over it, he tightly winds blue yarn 14 times around the top and bottom tassels and he knots it 2 or 3 times. Do this for each tassel until the *ojo de dios* is complete.

18. If you wish, you may trim the tassel ends. Antonio cut them to 1 inch, but such trimming is probably not done in the Huichol country where scissors are rare.

NEARIKA 2

The blazing colors and symbols of the *nearika* make it one of the most striking and brilliant crafts of Mexico today. The modern *nearika*, a yarn painting of the Huichol Indians, is derived partly from the ancient *tufa*, a decorated disc of volcanic ash used for votive offerings. It consists of colorful commercial yarns set in a base of *cera de Campeche*, the wild beeswax found in the crags and hollows of the Huicholes' precipitous land.

The creation of *nearikas* is both a ritual and a folk art. Interestingly enough, it was a folk art first. The Huicholes first wove the *nearikas* to trade with wandering peddlers. Eventually they found their way into the markets and are now sold throughout Mexico, particularly to tourists. Although others have taken up the craft, only the *nearika* of the Huichol is authentic; the others are copies or even fakes.

The ritualistic aspects of the *nearika* are very much influenced by peyote, the Huichol food for the soul. Sacred hunts are made yearly to San Luis Potosí, the land of the Huichol ancestors in the north central desert. Peyote is gathered and brought home for the pre-Conquest ceremony of the Burned *Máiz*, the annual burning of the corn fields. Through peyote the Huichol communes directly with his gods, but because its use is ritualistic, the Huichol does not take it all the time. To achieve his colors, he simply recalls what he has seen during previous rites.

The Huichol motifs used in the yarn paintings come from his history, his religion, and his visions (Figure 1). He chooses his symbols from a collection of sacred images that might include the horns of the deer, representing the prohibition against sexual relations with non-Huicholes; the heart of the deer, representing peyote; the deer itself, representing the sun; or the eagle. Great Grandmother Earth, Great Grandfather Deer Tail, Morning Star, Sun Father, and Grandmother Growth are all represented as themselves and by a series of their own symbols.

FIGURE 1

The way in which all of these symbols are used differs although the same symbols appear in both the ritual and the folk-art *nearikas*. For his folk-art *nearika*, the Huichol places the symbols in meaningless arrangements—he mixes them up. To the non-Huichol viewer they look fancifully logical. But for their ritualistic art, the symbols must be chosen so they pertain only to the god for whom the *nearika* is intended.

Athough the symbols are common property, the weaver's expression of each symbol is different. His choice of color is optional unless a particular myth requires certain sacred colors. The Huichol understands his colors and each *nearika* is as distinct as the hallucination that inspired it.

Just as the use of symbols differs in the folk-art and ritualistic *nearikas*, so does the actual method of construction. The ritual *nearika* is rounded at the corners and is always put on a wood backing. The folk-art *nearika* is often rectangular and is usually mounted on composition board, a material that is "Spanish," or foreign, and unacceptable to the gods.

The ritual *nearikas*, which are placed on the altars of temples and shrines, tell the legends of the Huichol gods such as the birth of the sun, the origin of corn, and the great flood. Some are similar to those of Judaic-Christian lore like that of Watakame who built a canoe when the world was drowned. Into the canoe he loaded a bitch, five grains of corn, five beans, and fire. When the dog became human, she and Watakame began to re-populate the world. They planted and ate the beans and corn, and with the fire they cooked and kept warm.

Some *nearikas* are exotic sagas. On a hot pink background, the treacherous path of the sexual transgressor is shown (see Figure 1). Male and female spirits who in life consorted at least once with a foreigner (a non-Huichol) are burdened with stylized sperm and ova on their five-day trip to the land of the dead; the females weighted with sperm, the males balancing vaginas or ova. They jounce and jostle these exaggerated symbols over a merry board, where they can retrace their steps and come out right—like a game. There is no eternal punishment. Finally these amusing ghost-like souls totter into a never-never land, free of the evidence of their lifetime sin and all is forgiven.

Whether ritualistic or folk art, the true Huichol *nearika* is a small spectacular. The imitations or fakes cannot possibly compete with the Huichol *nearika* which is truly bizarre.

Working with the Craftsman

TOOLS AND MATERIALS

Scissors.

Yarn. Use a three-ply wool, $\frac{1}{8}$ inch in diameter. Carpet or rug yarn, much of it produced in the United States, is a good medium and comes in all colors. As suggested in Chapter 1, stitchery skeins would be suitable for this craft because they come in $\frac{1}{4}$-ounce skeins. The *nearika* will require 2 or 3 ounces for the size given.

A twisted yarn gives a pleasing texture to the *nearika* (see Figure 13). Although synthetic yarn is suitable, real wool gives more texture and tends to expand, taking up "holidays." Get at least three colors: one to draw with, one to fill in with, and one to color the edge.

The Huichol children who made the demonstration *nearika* used four colors: royal blue, light blue, purple, and green—although they explained that a *nearika* should always have some reds and yellows in it if for no other reason than to make it prettier!

A strong thumbnail.

Plyboard. Buy enough thick plyboard for the *nearika* you wish to make. The model is approximately $8\frac{1}{2}$ by 11 inches. It is made of composition board, but plywood is preferable because it is a stronger backing and the oil from the wax will not seep through the wood.

Base wax. The Huicholes use *cera de Campeche*, a wax from a particular kind of bee that builds its combs in their high Sierra homeland. It is a bright yellow wax which is mixed with resin and brought by the Indians to the markets of Tepic, Guadalajara, and Zapopan.

Cera de Campeche has both advantages and disadvantages. The *nearika* requires a base that will remain pliable until the entire painting is completed. This wax provides a flexible base for the yarn and does not become too brittle, but its sensitivity to heat and cold can present problems. In the Huichol country, one cannot work with this wax on a cold day. If it becomes too hot, the wax begins to melt and seep into the yarn. The children usually work inside the church where the temperature is cool and even. Though the yarn may "insulate" the wax somewhat, it does not protect it entirely from weather changes. A *nearika* backed by *cera de Campeche* must always be kept out of direct sunlight and out of a hot room. When I brought the *nearika* back to San Miguel from Guadalajara by car, the oil of the wax seeped through the back of the composition board.

To avoid some of the difficulties presented by the *cera de Campeche*, use one of the following recipes to make your wax substitute. (You will still find, however, that your wax will react quickly to temperature changes. Best performance is achieved at a work-area temperature near 75°.)

a. In Mexico I used two $8\frac{1}{2}$-inch paraffin candles ($\frac{7}{8}$ inch in diameter), 100 grams of resin (3.5 ounces), and 22 grams of Vaseline (about 1 ounce).

b. In the United States I used a 4-ounce slab of paraffin (from the grocery store). Encountering difficulty finding "raw" resin (sold in hardware stores in Mexico), I substituted the cake rosin musicians use for rosining their bows. These cakes come in different sizes. I used three, a total of 4 ounces (though expensive, they worked). To this I added $\frac{1}{2}$ ounce of Vaseline.

c. Another possibility is to use 4 ounces of batik wax to which no resin need be added, and about $\frac{1}{4}$ ounce of Vaseline.

Whichever method you use, melt the paraffin in a double boiler first. (Never melt wax directly over a heat source.) Pulverize your resin if using recipe *a* or *b*. Add the liquid paraffin, stirring constantly with a wooden spoon until the resin is dissolved. Then add the Vaseline, stirring this until dissolved.

Allow the mixture to cool in the pan, or pour into crockery.

I waited until the next day and then set the pan in the sun so that the wax mixture would soften. Then I pried it out with a spoon and worked it into several fist-sized balls. These mixtures do not change as readily with the weather and neither are they so oily as the *cera de Campeche*. They should be workable and remain workable after very little kneading, provided that your working-area temperature is warm enough. You can substitute wax made in this manner for the *cera de Campeche* used in the directions which follow. Antonio Pineda makes a *nearika*:

PROCEDURE   *NEARIKA*

1. Since *cera de Campeche* is never softened by fire, Antonio places the wax in the Mexican sun which at high noon softens it to a   *23*

workable consistency in just five minutes. He kneads and works the wax with his fingers until it is a bit stickier than workable dough.

2. Now in the shade, Antonio applies the prepared wax to his board. With the board on his knee, he breaks off one large pinch of wax at a time. Holding the wax in one hand he applies it with the thumb of his other hand, pressing it hard. Turning the board and smoothing the edges as he works, Antonio spreads the wax about 3/16 inch thick in more or less the order shown in Figure 2. Antonio works away from himself as he spreads the wax. The wax does not have to be smooth. It looks like cool butter after it is spread (Figure 3).

FIGURE 2

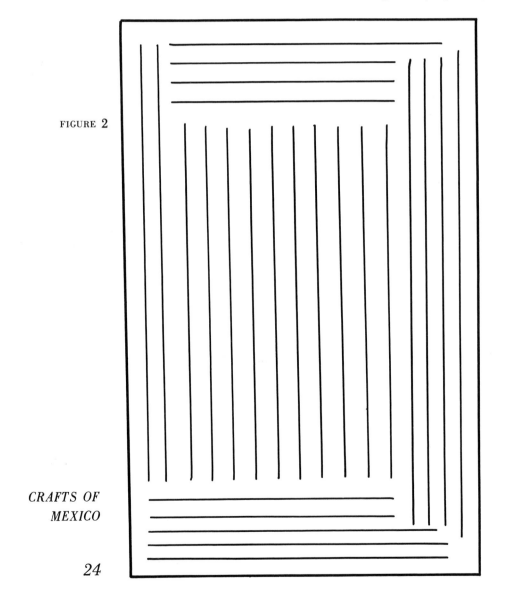

FIGURE 3

Before you cover the entire board, it is a good idea to experiment with the yarn on the wax. If the wax is too thin, the wool will not be held adequately; if it is too thick, the yarn may sink too far into it.

3. Now Antonio cuts straight across the end of some royal blue yarn and twists the end. The yarn ends are always twisted before using. He places one strand along the top edge of the waxed board. Pay careful attention to the application of the first strand. Do not round the corners; they will round themselves somewhat anyway. Be sure the yarn grabs well. If necessary, add more wax to the edges. There is a tendency to skimp here. Going around all four edges, Antonio presses the yarn into the wax about $\frac{1}{8}$ inch with his thumbnail.

Though Antonio did not have one, I have seen Huicholes from the mountain country who have grown extremely long thumbnails which evidently facilitate making a yarn painting. Antonio occasionally used his fingernail when his thumbs were tired, but the thumb is the real tool of the *nearika*.

4. Antonio continues making the second row inside the first row by pressing the yarn into the wax with his thumbnail. (Do not be

disturbed by nailprints, they are unavoidable and will not show later.) Hold the yarn taut at all times with one hand while you position it with the other. Place the yarn as close to the previously laid row as you can. Pay special attention to the corners. When you turn the yarn, never let it twist or overlap. The turns must be sharp and definite.

5. Antonio applies a third row of royal blue. By custom most *nearikas* have three colors bordering the edge. This one does not because only these colors were available that day.

6. Putting a skein of light blue yarn around his neck, Antonio cuts off the yarn end so it is straight and then twists the ends as he prepares to "draw" the figure—the *venado* or sacred deer. Although the design may be outlined with the thumbnail first, Antonio forms the design directly on the wax as he applies the yarn. Starting with the deer's back and going left, Antonio outlines the deer (Figure 4 and Plate 2). Its antlers are applied later.

7. He begins the second row of the deer's back next to the first, across the neck and around the body (Figure 5). He continues around the body and up into the tail for the second row in the tail.

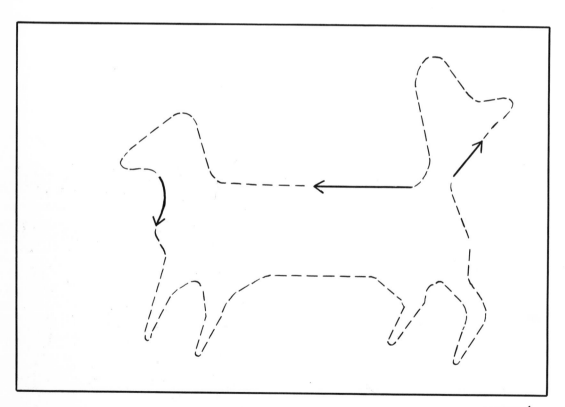

FIGURE 4

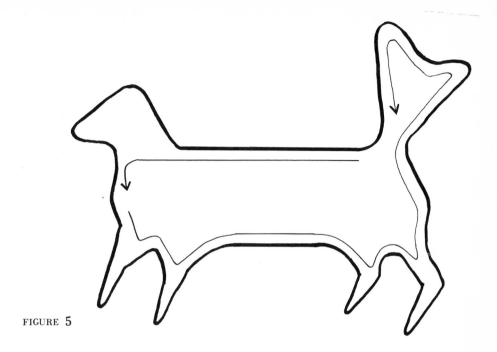

FIGURE 5

8. The third row of the body follows the second row across the deer's back and into the tail again, forming the third row of the tail (Figure 6).

9. The fourth and fifth rows also go into the tail. Antonio has been using one continuous strand of yarn. Remember to keep the yarn taut and place the strands close together. Make sharp, well-pressed-in turns. This is the secret of the texture of the pattern; the "waves" of the figures and the spaces of the *nearika*.

FIGURE 6

10. Antonio cuts the yarn in the tail after the fifth row. Remember never to overlap or cross the yarn. Cut whenever necessary, twist the yarn ends, and then continue with the new yarn.

11. Using newly cut and twisted yarn (still light blue), Antonio places the end inside the body. He makes several rows, leaving space for the purple center (Figure 7).

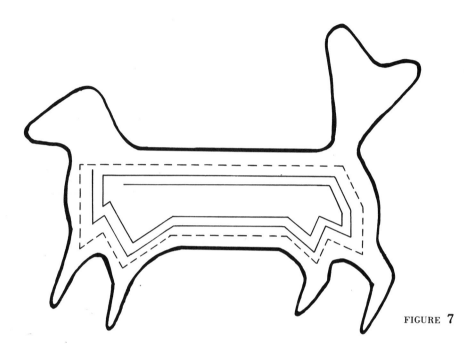

FIGURE 7

12. He then cuts the purple yarn end straight and fills in the central area of the deer's body. When it is completely enclosed, he cuts the yarn end and presses it in.

13. Taking royal blue yarn, he applies the deer's eye next, spiraling it in firmly, outside to inside.

14. Now the deer is finished except for the head and the tail. Antonio fills in the head with light blue yarn. When he cannot go around the entire head anymore, he fills in the area that remains between the eye and the jaw (Figure 8).

15. He makes light blue antlers next. Beginning at the lower right (Figure 9), he presses one continuous line: up, around, down, across; up, around, down, across, etc., until both antlers have been shaped and he is back where he began.

16. Now Antonio fills in the tail with royal blue (see Figure 13). The order presented here is the order in which the deer was made, but

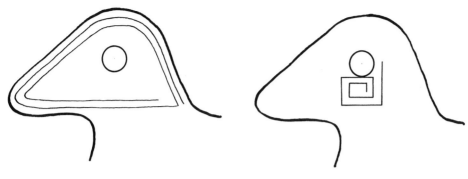

FIGURE 8

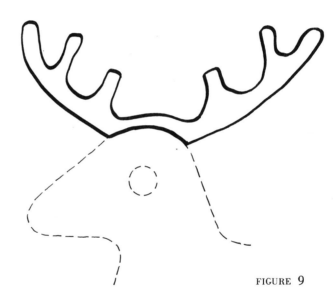

FIGURE 9

the center of the body and the center of the tail can be applied whenever the opportunity presents itself.

17. Antonio puts in the background using bright green yarn. Figure 10 is merely a guide to show the general method of applying the background. The tautness of the yarn and the sharpness of the corners are more important in the large areas than the application sequence. In general these areas are filled in logically. Follow the instructions below and refer to Figure 10:

Area 1 Put the yarn around the right antler, the deer's back, and the tail (Figure 11).

NEARIKA

29

FIGURE 10

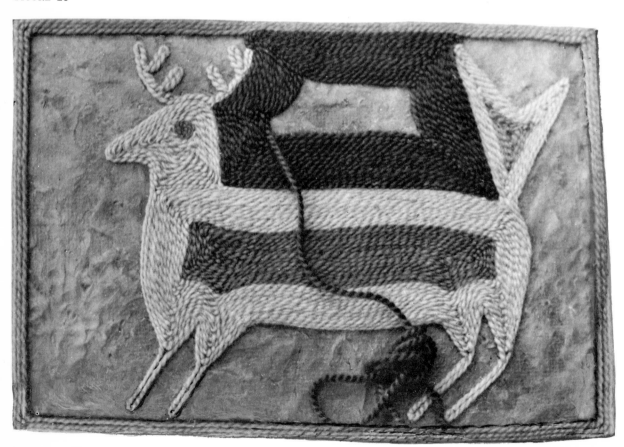

FIGURE 11

FIGURE **12**

FIGURE **13**

Area 2 Filling in the area between the antlers (Figure 12) requires more patience and a long thumbnail is helpful.

Area 3 Filling in the area between the front of the deer and the border is easier. Antonio laid down two strands at a time. (Sometimes on larger *nearikas* as many as four strands are applied at once, but they must be applied straight and evenly, and this takes considerable experience.) This was the first time Antonio noticeably squeezed the yarn to fit. It was done so that the same filament could be used to fill in the constricted area between the deer's nose and the border.

Area 4 This was filled in with a continuous strand as long as it was feasible to do so and then the area above the tail was completed with a separate piece.

Area 5 The lower background was filled in the same way until it was no longer possible to do with one strand. At this point, Antonio filled in the area between the two forelegs and then applied the rest of the area (Figure 13).

Because your drawing and the application of yarn will not work out in precisely the same way the model did—no two *nearikas* are ever alike—it is necessary only to follow the concept of the yarn application: fill in a logical open area with one continuous strand until you can no longer do so. Then start a new area.

NEARIKA

31

3 *SERAPE*

Weaving is one of Mexico's, as well as one of the world's, oldest crafts and the *serape* or blanket is one of the finest examples of the craft as it is practiced in Mexico.

The traditional *serape* worn only by the man—the *campesino*—is a wool blanket. It is his overcoat, his blanket, and reportedly his wedding cloak. It is a covering of a thousand uses. With a slit in the center, it is worn over his body to keep him warm in the high cold country. Folded over his shoulder, it is a decoration. The *serape*, handwoven from costly wool is a treasure which will last for many years, and for some, a lifetime. Finally, the *serape* will be his shroud. The sophisticated may use the *serape* as a rug, a blanket, a bedspread, or a decorative furniture or wall covering. For all, it is a prized possession.

Serapes are woven in all parts of the country, although in the colonial era it was said that the town of Saltillo made the best. The town of San Miguel de Allende, however, in the state of Gunanjuato, was cited as its equal. San Miguel is the home of the Amaros, one of several families of weavers. "We have been here since the beginning," said David Amaro. Weaving has been their family tradition for at least 300 years.

The craft began in San Miguel in the seventeenth or eighteenth century. No one knows. Like the other regions of Mexico, San Miguel is known for its particular weaving patterns. No one really knows exactly where they came from or how they began. During the Revolution of 1910 and the chaotic times that followed, some of the patterns were almost forgotten, but the old styles and techniques of San Miguel survived and are carried on today. Francisco Vargas, an old man in 1939, was one who remembered the old patterns. He had begun weaving as a child, perhaps toward the end of the 1860's. Today, his student, Felix Pérez Juarez, carries on those traditions. Many of the old styles such as the *San Miguel, las jesuses, las copas* (cups), *las trenzas* (braids), *la culebra* (snake), *los jamonsillos* (candies), *la pluma de águila* (plume of the eagle) were patterns that originated in San Miguel. And there were more: *centros de San Miguel, palmas de San Miguel,* and others. Some were popular patterns for *cobijas,* bed and sofa coverings used on the ranches. Some were patterns for rugs.

The old San Miguel patterns are a mixture of Indian, Spanish, and Moorish influences. They are geometrics made of interlocking diamonds, zigzags, and variations of triangles and polygons. Some figures are built into complicated arrangements while others give the illusion of depth through the use of color. Variations of the Greek key, called the *grecas* were also incorporated into woven designs. This historically universal symbol is found on some of Mexico's pyramids and was used extensively in pre-Conquest design. The patterns on solid backgrounds utilizing birds, ducks, and fish came into use only within the last thirty years.

San Miguel is still a center for weaving today. Felipe Cocio Pomar, a Peruvian who founded the first Belles Arts school in San Miguel in 1938, encouraged a revival of the arts here. In weaving, new designs were begun and old ones were revived. Today the school lives again as part of the National School of Fine Arts. Felix Pérez, disciple of Francisco Vargas, is its Professor of Weaving and Textiles. Two other schools in San Miguel also teach weaving and there are so many weaver's shops throughout the town that one can often glimpse through open doorways and see brilliantly colored yarn drying in the clean air.

Thirty or forty years ago the Street of the Chorro was the street of the weavers. On market day the *tejedores* or weavers sat in their doorways displaying the woven wares they had for sale. Early each morning the weavers could be seen at the Chorro, the waterworks of the town, where they rinsed their dyed wool. Calle Nuñez was the street of the *cambaya* weavers, the weavers of cotton, and Montes de

Occa was the street of the *rebozos* (the long rectangular "shawl" worn by the country women of Mexico). Here women made as much as 40 to 80 centavos for each delicately knotted strand of the fringe of the *rebozo,* a job that often was farmed out.

The weaving of ancient Mexico was extravagant and magnificent. When Moctezuma met Cortés in 1519, he descended from a litter whose canopy was entwined with green feathers of the hummingbird and embroidered with gold and silver; pearls and jade were suspended from its tasseled edge. He wore a *tilmatl,* a fine cotton cloak encrusted with emeralds, jade, and other precious stones. Under the cloak he wore a *maxtlatl,* or loincloth, intricately designed and bordered with deep fringe. His sandals of gold touched only the cotton cloth that was strewn before him so that his royal feet might never touch the ground. His *caciques,* or noblemen, wore rich mantles of featherwork or elegant embroidery each different from the other. Moctezuma presented Cortés with many gifts: robes of finely woven plumes and furs and cotton cloth, some as fine as silk, some interwoven with feathers and animal hair.

These gifts as well as the dress of Moctezuma himself were indicative of pre-Conquest Mexican weaving in which materials of all types were used to adorn the wealthy (Figure 1). Plumage from the quetzal, the toucan, the macaw, and other tropical birds were inserted in the web of the cloth with their tips exposed to produce an irridescent sheen. Shields were woven and armor of quilted cotton was adorned with gold, silver, and precious stones. Aristocratic maidens were taken to live in the *teocallis,* the religious houses of the great temples, where they did fine weaving. Wealthy women spent many tranquil hours at their spinning and fine embroidery. Weaving on a more basic level was done in almost every household where women spun cotton for the family's clothing.

Working on a horizontal loom, the pre-Conquest Indian used cotton, magey, and other fibers. Their complicated patterns were woven directly into the cloth in the same way designs are incorporated into the *serape* today, although generally the pre-Conquest materials were much more refined than those currently in use. Innumerable design motifs were utilized but all were stylized geometric representations of nature; birds, animals, fish, flowers, suns, and moons all had religious significance.

Just as many of the same designs are used today, so the ancient backstrap or horizontal loom is found in many parts of Mexico today.

FIGURE 1

In Oaxaca one can watch a weaver making a *huipil*, the ancient Mexican blouse that is sometimes lengthened to a dress. The backstrap loom which she uses is attached to a heavy woven belt around her waist (Figure 1A). The warp thread is stretched between two sticks and the other end is attached to a tree. Because the width of the cloth one can weave is limited with this kind of loom, the finished *huipil* consists of six panels: three in front and three in back, each about 10 inches wide.

Although the designs and sometimes the weaving techniques are the same, today's weaver rarely uses the natural colors that were used before and even after the Conquest. These natural colors included cochineal, a scarlet made from a parasitic insect; dark blue from

SERAPE

35

the *anil*, an indigo plant; and black from the seed of a tropical tree. Purple was obtained from *caracoles*, mollusks found on the Pacific coast. Called murex, these mollusks still are gathered in southern Oaxaca and in Guerrero by the Amusgo and Chontal Indians, but they are usually used for the indigenous population; murex-dyed products are rarely sold "outside."

Handweaving continued into the middle of the nineteenth century when the Industrial Revolution brought the first large textile mill to Mexico. Although the mills introduced large scale automated weaving procedures to Mexico, the natural colored *manta*, the coarse cottons, the belts, the *huipiles*, the *rebozos*, the *bolsas* (bags or purses), and the *serapes* were and still are woven by hand. The dyed *cambaya* is is demand too, by the tourist who buys "resort" clothes of this cloth, hand embroidered in fanciful adapted pre-Conquest patterns.

The Spanish introduction of the upright loom and the use of wool began the Indian tradition of *serape* weaving—a latecomer on the Mexican scene. The *serape* replaced the *tilmatl* or *tilma*, the pre-Conquest cloak. Women took up the Spanish-Moorish custom of *rebozo* weaving. The Spanish also brought the spinning wheel. Until then the clay whorl and spinning stick were used.

The Amaro family and the other San Miguel *serape* weavers began their craft sometime after the Conquest. Today, four members of the family continue the tradition as *tejedores* or weavers in a colonial house which serves as their workshop or *taller*. Built on a steep hill, this large house extends right up to the street in the Spanish manner. Skeins of yarn hang in the red brick courtyards where small trees grow and flowers bloom.

On the lower level an electric carding machine dominates one dark room. It is the only motor-driven machine in the entire workshop. The looms are foot-operated and all the other processes are done by hand.

The principal work areas are on the upper levels. Under a small tile roof the wool is dyed in a large stone brazier heated by a wide gas jet running through the oven. For thirty minutes the wool is dyed in great tubs occasionally stirred with a wooden stick. The colors the Amaros use are aniline dyes imported from the United States.

Before it is dyed, the wool is washed with soap and water in large cement tubs located a few steps above the dyeing level. We watched one of the helpers wash the raw wool that had been brought in from ranches near Dolores Hidalgo, a town not far from San Miguel. The natural wool, in black, gray, and white, is washed and rewashed before it is hung to dry.

As we continued to the next level we found a smaller workroom containing only two looms. "These looms are over one hundred years old," said Sr. Amaro as we watched the *tejedor* weave a geometric pattern of various greens. He showed us a beautifully carved *lanzadero* or shuttle, made of dark brown wood. "It is eighty years old," he said.

In an adjacent workroom, five looms, one of them double-sized, were crowded together—a common situation. The weaver rarely experiences good working conditions. He works long hours in small, dark, cramped spaces and rarely does anything to change it for it is the custom; his family has worked in the same way and the same place for hundreds of years.

Yarn is stored and draped everywhere—all colors, all intensities, some brilliant and vibrant, others muted. In the larger workroom, Sr. Amaro's nephew was weaving a round *serape* of structured diamonds in orange, burnt orange, and brown. He was making the San Miguel. The thick, closely woven *serape* would be six feet in diameter and would take four days to complete.

The colors used in the *serape* are a good example of the various influences that affect crafts today. When a San Miguel-based decorator first went to the Amaros, she found that their techniques were good, but their colors were garish. The decorator, therefore, provided samples of the colors that she wanted and the Amaros produced them. This experience continued to influence their work and enhance their products. They adapted the new ideas to the old traditions. The Amaro's experience was a fortunate one. Commercial influences are often detrimental as can be seen in Mexico City's elite shopping areas where gaudy as well as fine *serapes* are offered for sale together.

Natural colors are seldom used today by the "commercial" weavers. Not long ago, I watched a weaver in San Miguel who had come in from the country for market day. He was carrying four, thick *serapes* of natural gray wool. When he spread them on the sidewalk near the plaza, I saw they were accented by three broad stripes of jolting hot pink. The craftsman is an artist, but he must also live. He must make what the customer demands. In the highlands, the weavers still make the ancient, natural wool *serape* for the native population, but they are difficult to find or not for sale.

Moctezuma's descendents no longer weave the flowing mantles of featherwork; the brilliant *quetzals* have been protected by law for years. The refined weaving of gold and silver with plumes or embedded precious stones is a lost art. (Some weaving with metallic thread is going on in Mexico City, but is a pseudo-Mexican craft, a sophisticated craft done mainly by foreigners.)

But many still weave in the old way in the patterns of the ancients: the birds, the flowers, the stylized creatures, the suns, the moons, the geometrics. Amaro's nephew weaves on the Spanish-brought upright loom with the Spanish-brought wool, the old patterns, a mixture of the Indian and the Spanish, the patterns that have become traditional to San Miguel.

Working with the Craftsman

Fidel Hernandez Méndez is the craftsman who weaves the San Miguel for us. He is a master weaver who had been a *tejedor* at the Bellas Artes in the early years. Next to him a *tejedor* is weaving a modern rug by following a small, intricate pattern that is tacked on the frame of the loom.

Whereas the Amaro *taller* is a family enterprise, Lucha Mojica employs others. Perhaps fifteen people work here; some only card the wool (which is done by hand), others wash and dye the yarn. A sales office is at the front of the compound where a secretary is employed.

The Mojica *serapes* and *tapetes* (large rugs) are sold all over the world. They are among the finest made anywhere. The Mojicas also maintain a shop in Bazar Sábado in Mexico City.

The looms here, measured by the size *serape* they hold, are 1, 2, and $2\frac{1}{4}$ meters wide. Although they can be woven any size, this San Miguel is woven on a 1-meter loom. The upright loom is a large wood frame on which two large spools are mounted. The warp strings are wound onto the front spool. As the *serape* is woven, it is wound onto the back spool (the larger spool closer to the weaver).

The men at the *taller* work quickly. Their fingers synchronize with the movement of the pedals which set two pulleys in action. These pulleys raise and lower two pairs of horizontal sticks to which are strung vertical crisscross strings. These strings separate the warp threads so the *lanzadero* (the shuttle) or the *mariposa* (wound yarn) can be inserted through alternating warp threads to make the weft pattern.

The beater, also holding vertical threads (but not the warp threads), is pulled toward the weaver to tighten the weave after each weft weave across the width of the loom.

To watch how the *serape* is actually made, we went to the *taller* of Lucha Mojica, cousin of José Mojica (see Chapter 9). Here, the light was better for taking photographs and there was more room to move in and out between the looms than there was at the Amaro workshop. The looms were still close together, however, and it was difficult to watch the weavers at work because the observer constantly had to keep out of the way of the beaters slamming against the weave.

Preparation of the Wool

Before being woven, wool is subjected to many preparatory operations. The following procedures are practiced at the *taller* of Lucha Mojica in San Miguel de Allende:

When the wool is brought to the *taller* from surrounding ranches, it has already been separated according to natural colors and packed

FIGURE 2

FIGURE 3

into loosely woven burlap bags. It is placed in a basket and put into outdoor *pilas* or water tanks. The basket containing the wool floats in the pure water while the wool is washed (Figures 2 and 3). When it is clean, it is spread to dry.

The wool is then carded or shredded like wispy cotton mat. Throughout Mexico most carding is done by hand, a process which takes many hours. At Amaro's it was done electrically, but the Mojica's do it by hand.

Next the wool is spun into yarn on a hand-operated spinning wheel and the yarn is washed with soap. When it is dry, it is wound into skeins, *madejas*, on a reel. (A skein is approximately ½ kilo or about 1 pound.) At this point, the yarn that will not be left a natural color is ready to be dyed. German aniline dyes, Citocol, are used (the use of native vegetable dyes is rare). While the dye is being prepared, the wool is soaked in another tub of water. The skeins are all tied together at one end. To prepare the dye, a wood fire is built in the open brick oven. High temperatures are maintained by adding clumps of discarded wool saturated with kerosene and by adding more wood when necessary. Six boxes of dye (1 box per skein), 400 grams of rocksalt (about 14 ounces), and about 40 liters of water (or enough water to cover the wool) are combined in large tin tubs that are heated on the oven. The yarn is put into the dye after it comes to a full boil. For 30 minutes the wool in this steaming, foaming solution is poked, stirred, lifted, and separated with a long stick (Figure 4). (Black dye takes one hour. All other colors require 30 minutes except when 12 skeins rather than 6 are dyed at once, in which case 45 minutes is required.)

When ready, the skeins are lifted out at one time and set on the clean rock patio where they are separated and hung for a few minutes. One by one, they are rinsed in three vats of water and then wrung. The yarn is hung in the courtyard until it is dry and ready to be woven.

FIGURE 4

An upright, 2-harness loom that is strung singly at 6 warp threads per inch with four sets of four strings at each side to strengthen the selvedge.

The warp thread is a heavy, white cotton string.

Yarn. Six colors were used in the model (Plate 3): wine, yellow, olive green, bright green, and two natural wools, one white and one a dark, almost black, brown. I chose these colors from a *serape* the Mojicas use in their house. The colors seemed Moorish and, therefore, appropriate. The colors you choose may be completely different, and you may want to use fewer. The San Miguel can be made in any colors, but you must use at least five and no more than eight.

The size of the yarn is a mystery. I could not find its equal in the United States. It is not a ply but a thick, dense yarn (about $\frac{1}{8}$ inch in diameter). A skein weighs about one pound, but each skein is a slightly different length. The weavers only estimate how much yarn they will need of each color. No one knows exactly how much. When finished, the model weighed two pounds, about one-third of which was yellow yarn, one-third wine, and one-third composed of the remaining colors.

Mexican handspun wool is available through several sources. Ecuadorian wool is similar and also available.

Templero, a template.

A Spinning wheel or some other device for winding the many *mariposas*.

Razor blade.

A few sheets of $8\frac{1}{2}$-by-11 inch blank or squared *paper.*

Pencils and colored pencils.

Felt pens in the same colors as the wool.

PROCEDURE FOR DIAGRAM

As far as Lucha Mojica knew, no one outside San Miguel has ever woven the San Miguel *serape* and even there only professional weavers and a few adventurous and advanced weaving students have tried it. No diagrams or plans are available in San Miguel. They are unnecessary because the weavers have memorized this complicated motif. After reading the directions, if you feel the design is too complicated see Step 8. It took Fidel approximately 15 hours to make this *serape*.

1. It is absolutely necessary to make a diagram for this pattern. If you look at the *serape* as if the yellow and not the wine were dominant it will be easier to dissect the pattern. The completed *serape* is made in what is called the *vaciado* technique. This means that the entire pattern is composed of diamonds or diagonals.

Work out the pattern on a small sheet of paper first. Cut an 8½-by-11-inch sheet to 7 1/3-by 11 inches.

2. Fold the paper horizontally into eighths. Notice that the first and last horizontal sections of the *serape* are divided into half-diamonds by the brown and wine border. To allow for this division, fold the first and last eighths of your paper in half.

3. Next fold the paper vertically into quarters. Since the borders must be equal all around the pattern, measure the half fold that you made at the top (or bottom) of your paper; mark this measurement on both lateral sides of your paper, and then fold (Figure 5). This will give you a 2 to 3 proportion—the proportion that is used throughout the *serape*.

4. Now that the paper is folded, begin to draw the diagram in pencil following the example in Figure 6.

5. Although the actual measurements of the model are given here, it is the proportion that counts rather than the measurements. The proportion is 2 to 3. The proposed *serape* was to be 26 by 39 inches. The actual *serape* turned out to be 28 by 42 inches. The discrepancy was unimportant since a proportion of 2 to 3 was maintained.

Though the *serape* was woven on a 1-meter loom, the warp strings are strung a little differently each time. You must determine the actual width of your warp strings to weave this *serape* correctly. Because this is a symmetrical design, Fidel assures me that the pattern will not turn out evenly if the weaver does not keep to the 2 to 3 proportion. Fidel measured the *serape* after he had begun weaving the pattern to determine its actual size.

Again, think of the wine as the background and the yellow as the dominant pattern. Think of the brown triangles in the pattern as borders for the yellow. The white figures fit into the center of the yellow and the center of each part of the wine background.

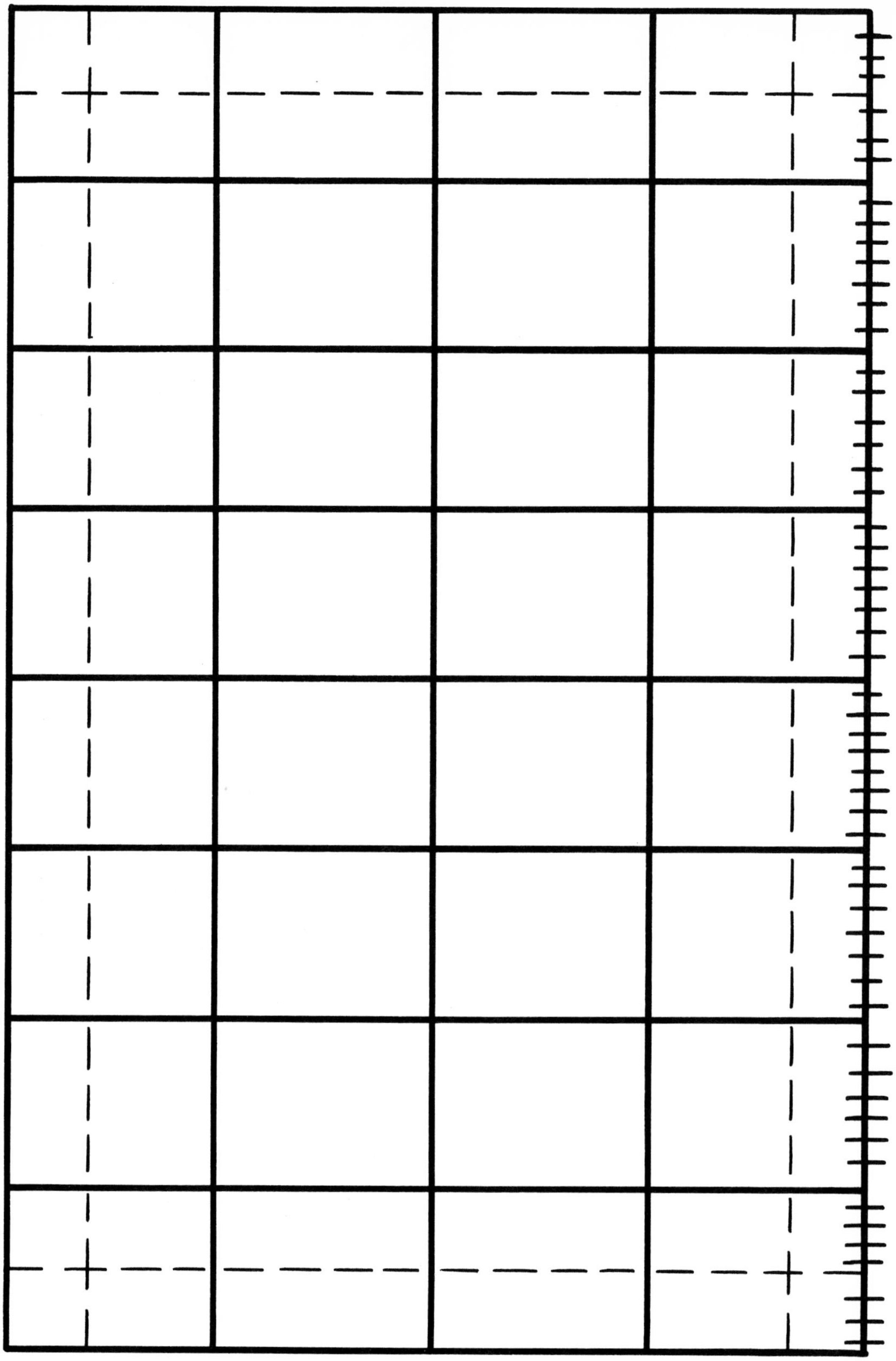

FIGURE 5

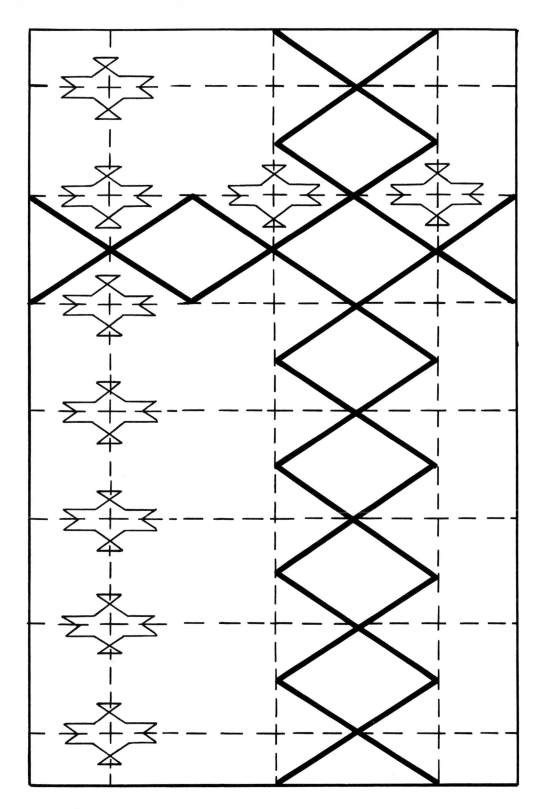

FIGURE 6

The border is $1\frac{1}{2}$ inches of dark brown and 1 inch of wine. You will have half-diamonds all the way around the border, each pointing inward. The pattern across the *serape* takes up 23 inches and lengthwise, 37 inches. The number of yellow patterns across is $\frac{1}{2} + 1 + 1 + \frac{1}{2}$. Lengthwise, they are $\frac{1}{2} + 1 + 1 + 1 + 1 + 1 + 1 + \frac{1}{2}$. The white figures in the wine number 3 across and 7 down. In the yellow they contain a center of bright green; in the wine they have a center of olive. These forms are called *cacahuates* (peanuts). Actually, this form is repeated throughout the pattern.

Although measuring is useless, the reader can work out this pattern by knowing how many warp strings he has and then working out the pattern from there or, he can use graph paper if the number of vertical lines on the paper corresponds to the number of warp strings on the loom. Also, be sure you have the right number of horizontal lines for your 2 to 3 proportion.

Work your diagram with pencil until everything fits (Figures 7 through 13). Keep looking at it from one point of view. It is easy for the eye to begin to see other patterns and if you begin to follow them, confusion will set in.

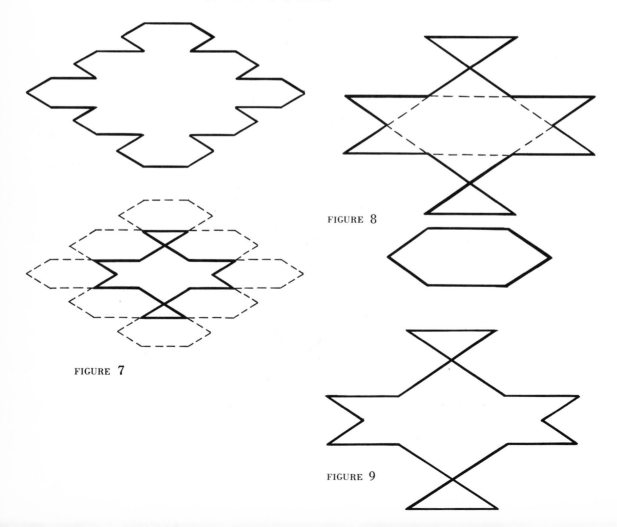

FIGURE 7

FIGURE 8

FIGURE 9

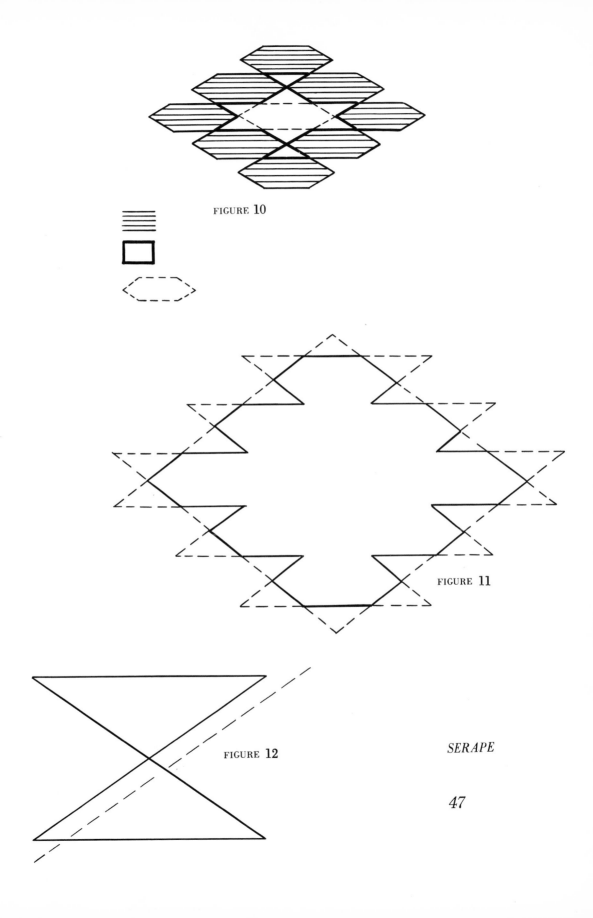

FIGURE 10

FIGURE 11

FIGURE 12

SERAPE

47

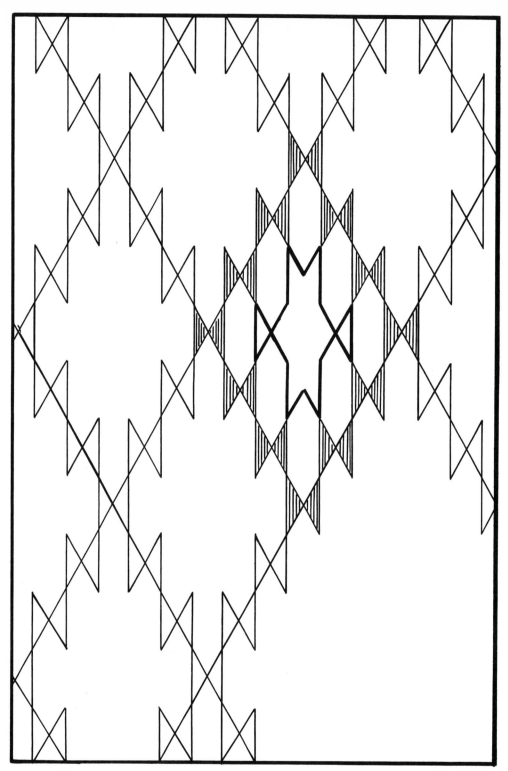

FIGURE 13

6. After you have made the diagram to get the feel of the pattern, do what the *tejedores* do. Transfer the small pattern to a large sheet of heavy brown paper cut to the size of the finished *serape*. Then outline the pattern in the correct colors. Remember to measure the width of your warp for the actual size.

Place this pattern beneath the vertical strings (the warp) of the loom and reproduce the pattern again. But this time, draw it directly on the warp strings. Though they used only one color to draw the pattern at the *taller*, I suggest you use colored felt pens. This will greatly simplify your weaving. You will not have to stop constantly to figure out what color comes next. Confusion and the chance of error will be minimized. Once this is done, the greatest difficulty is past. You have only to follow this pattern on the warp as you weave. You can check your pattern by making sure the design and the colors are equal on each side.

7. Once the pattern is transferred to the loom and you begin to weave, it is necessary to look at the pattern differently. Try to see it layer by layer, or thread by thread while at the same time seeing the whole pattern. For instance, the first row of the beginning of the pattern is started by the insertion of the *mariposas* in this order: green, yellow, yellow, green, yellow, yellow, green, yellow, yellow, green. But actually all that must be done from this point on is to follow the color pattern you have drawn on your strings. You will be adding and deleting colors with each row according to the design. The horizontal patterns (diamonds) grow and diminish with each weave (Figure 14).

FIGURE **14**

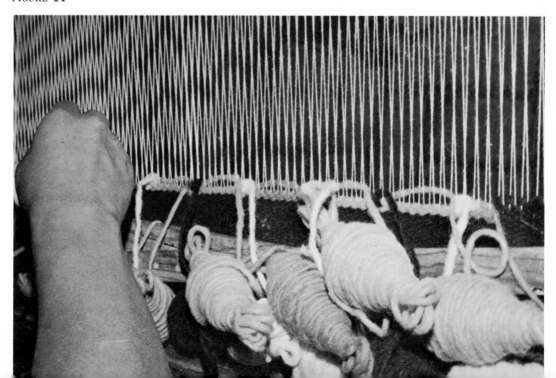

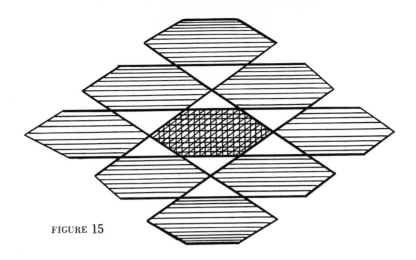

FIGURE 15

Do not be concerned if each side or each figure is not perfect. They are sometimes not perfect even when master weavers do them. This is handwork; it is only the machine that weaves perfectly. One of the weavers said, "It takes one who really knows how to weave to be able to do the ancient styles. We begin to learn by carding the wool. Gradually we work up to the loom. It is two or three years before we are entrusted with the old patterns—they are the most difficult."

8. A much simpler variation of the San Miguel is one large figure in the center of a solid background. This, while not the true San Miguel, is within the reach of anyone who has ever woven. The true San Miguel will take an experienced weaver. The *serape* I saw of this simpler design contained *cacahuates* of hot pink, a center of orange, and white stars all on a field of bright aqua. Any colors can be used. If you weave this *serape* think from the *cacahuate* point of view (Figure 15). But whether or not you choose to weave the complicated pattern or the simplified one, the diagram is still the key.

PROCEDURE FOR WEAVING.

1. The yarn is wound onto the *canillas* and the *mariposas* first. The *canilla* is the spool inserted into the shuttle which is used only for the top and the bottom of this *serape* (see Figure 17). Except for the top and the bottom borders, all the San Miguel is woven with *mariposas*. The *mariposa* is not wound on a spool but is yarn that is wound on yarn. Make a "spool" of yarn about 8 inches long, then

FIGURE 16

loosely wind the rest of the yarn around this artificial "spool" (see Figures 16 and 19).

Mariposas are sometimes wound on outstretched fingers in a cross-wind. The result looks like a butterfly and thus the name, *mariposa.*

Wind the *mariposas* by the first method so that the yarn will not tangle easily. One of the greatest difficulties in weaving the San Miguel is keeping the *mariposas* from snarling and twisting.

2. The *lanzadero* (shuttle) is used only when the same color is used across the loom, when the color is solid, and when there is no design (Figure 17). The *mariposa* which is inserted by hand is used

FIGURE 17

to weave the design itself. Fidel lifts the correct number of strings with his fingers as he works the pedals of the loom. If the *mariposa* is still thick, he inserts it farther up in the shed where there is more space.

3. The weavers estimate how many *canillas* and *mariposas* they will need. Although he does not make them all before he begins, Fidel makes a good many. He starts by winding 1 *canilla* of heavy white string for the bottom edge of the *serape*. Then he winds 3 *canillas* of wine, and 4 or 5 of dark brown. He makes 13 *mariposas* of wine, 7 in olive, 12 in yellow, and several in white. Many more will be used before he is finished. Fidel calculates how much he will need by estimating each *mariposa* to contain 20 meters of yarn. Each is about 3 inches in diameter.

4. The *serape* is begun by using strong cotton string the same as that used for the warp.

Always make a large inverted "V" across the loom with the yarn when inserting it with the *lanzadero*. This keeps the yarn from being too tight when it is brought down against the weave with the beater (see Figure 20). You will have 10 rows of white string, then $1\frac{1}{2}$ inches of brown, and almost 1 inch of wine for the border. The brown and wine border will continue around the *serape*, but the lateral border will be inserted with the *mariposas*. You will begin and end each row with these same measurements of the brown and the wine. The white is used only at the top and the bottom of the *serape*.

In Mexico, the weaving is done with yarn prepared by hand. Its thickness and weight is, therefore, not standard. This creates a problem especially when the *mariposas* are used. The weaver needs skill and experience to judge the density of his yarn by sight and touch. When weaving the lateral brown and wine edging, Fidel found that the brown and the wine were not equal. He had to compensate by making additional weaves of the wine to equal the brown which was thicker.

5. After weaving the solid borders of brown and wine, the yarn inserted by the *mariposa* always overlaps (dovetails). For instance, when the brown and wine meet in the weave they are twined around the the same warp thread. The same is true for all the colors that meet (Figure 18). If this overlapping is not done, you will find you have a number of separate little rugs when finished.

6. After the first few inches of the *serape* are woven, Fidel inserts the *templero*, or template. This keeps the sides of the rug even

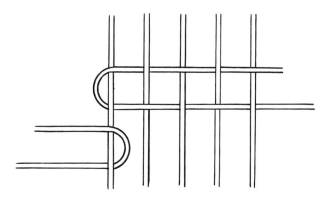

FIGURE 18

and is used throughout the weaving of the *serape*. It is moved when necessary (see Figure 20).

7. Beginning the design, he inserts the yarn from each *mariposa* for each part of the pattern whenever the color changes across the loom. He inserts the *mariposa* between the warp strings in the same way the *lanzadero* is begun.

A different *mariposa* is used for each part of the design even though the colors may be repeated. Therefore, in the first row, though only green and yellow are used, 10 *mariposas* are inserted in the order already mentioned: green, yellow, yellow, green, yellow, yellow, green, yellow, yellow, green. In the second row, 6 white and 3 brown *mariposas* are added and so on. You will be using many *mariposas* at one time before you are finished adding and deleting them as necessary (Figure 19).

FIGURE 19

If you run out of yarn, simply begin a new *mariposa,* overlapping the yarn a little in the weave. When Fidel no longer needs a color for a while, he simply cuts the yarn with a razor blade and sets the *mariposa* aside until he wants it again.

8. As in weaving with the *lanzadero,* when you use the *mariposa,* make a slight loop for each weave, no matter how short. This prevents the yarn from becoming too tight (see Figure 14).

9. Fidel weaves all the way across the loom using as many *mariposas* as he needs. Then he brings down the beater, banging it against the new weave three or four times, or as many times as necessary. Weaving back the other way, he uses the beater again. The sound of the beaters being brought against the weave is the sound of the weaver's workshop.

10. He continues weaving, winding more *mariposas* when necessary. Every so often he measures his work, making sure he is keeping to the proportions. (This should not be necessary for the reader who will have his pattern on the warp strings.)

11. At the end of the pattern, Fidel weaves wine, brown, and the white string using the *lanzadero* again for the border (Figure 20). He knots the end of the cotton weft to the warp string before cutting (Figure 21) and then cuts the warp leaving 6 inches of string (Figure 22).

As he cuts it, he loosely ties the warp (several strings at a time) while still on the loom so it will not become tangled.

Then he continues to wind the *serape* around the end spool until the *serape* rolls off (Figure 23). Usually a space is left and the *serape* is not removed until all the warp thread has been used. Four or five *serapes* can be woven on one set of warp strings.

FIGURE 20

FIGURE 21

FIGURE 22

FIGURE 23

12. Another man does the tying. (Though the following is the traditional method of tying San Miguel *serapes*, they could simply be knotted twice leaving the fringe free.) He takes two sets of 4 strings (remember that 4 sets of 4 have been strung for the selvedge at both the beginning and the end of the warp) and ties them twice, knotting them next to the weave, not at the tip. He takes the next 2 sets of 4 strings and ties them in the same way.

13. Then he takes the remaining threads by 2's, so that he has 2 sets of 2 threads, and knots them into sets of 4. He does this until he reaches the last 4 sets of 4 strings, where he repeats Step 12. (Figure 24).

FIGURE 24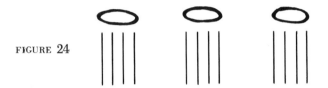

14. After he completes the initial knotting, he braids the 2 sets of 8 strings at the beginning (and later, at the end of the *serape*) within themselves. In other words, with eight strings, he will braid $3 + 3 + 2$ strings together; two times at the beginning and 2 times at the end of the *serape*. Each set is braided 6 times, then knotted twice (Figure 25).

FIGURE 25

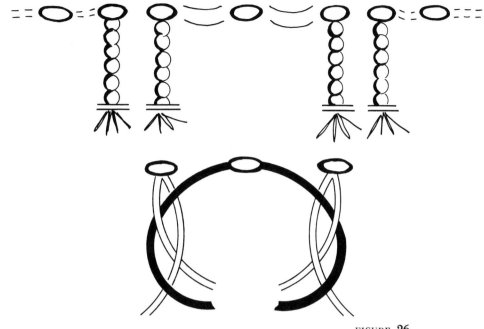

FIGURE **26**

15. Now he braids each of the three sets of 2 strings together (6 times) also knotting each braid twice as he completes it. These braids make a horizontal string pattern across the *serape* (Figure 26).

16. After the final knotting, the extra fringe is trimmed with a razor blade.

17. Another person cleans the *serape*, removing the foreign debris, the shards, and the bits of brush and burr that the sheep had picked up in their wanderings—some still not removed until now. Yet another person brushes the *serape* with *zacate*, a brush made of dried grasses or reeds. Finally, the stray strands of wool are snipped off.

The San Miguel is complete.

SERAPE

PART

II

REEDS

PETATE 4

Someone once remarked that wherever there is water in Mexico, there is also *petate* (mat) and basket weaving. This is certainly true of Ihuatzio, a town high in the mountain country of Michoacán on the shores of Lake Pátzcuaro. Here hundreds of *petateros*, weavers of reed mats, live and work.

During the months from May to November, the *petateros* are busy gathering the wild tule which grows in thickets along the cold, calm waters of Lake Pátzcuaro. Because the plant freezes and dies during the winter months, the weaver must gather a supply sufficient to last all year. Using a canoe made from a scooped-out log, the *petatero* glides through the tall reeds cutting them with a long-handled sickle. When he lands at his home shore, he straps the tule on his back and walks several kilometers to his house (Figure 1). Here he stores a supply of reeds in the rafters where they will be readily available when he needs them (Figure 2).

The *petate* craftsman, Plácido Hernandez-Ramirez lives in a simple but pleasant house surrounded by his corn stand and three ancient avocado trees. Hens and roosters scurry around the yard near his work area. "This week I weave the *petates*," he said. "Next week I will plant wheat. I am a *petatero*, a farmer, and a fisherman.

61

FIGURE 1

FIGURE 2

Most of the people here do more than one work. Those who do not own land, those who only weave, live in poverty."

Sr. Hernandez-Ramirez is one of the many hundreds of *petateros* in Ihuatzio. Walking through the town one can hear the tap-tap of these *petateros* at work as they pound their reed with stone. This craft is probably the humblest of all Mexican crafts, for the *petate* (Figure 20; Plates 4 and 5) is the object of the common man. These reed mats are used for sitting, sleeping, and eating. Babies are born on *petates* and the poor are buried in them. The craftsman who makes a *petate* often carries his wares wrapped in it, and then displays them on the same mat. (Plate 4). Because it is a symbol of the poor, it is often shunned by those who have "moved up." Those who have "arrived" may use it again decoratively, but not as the utilitarian thing it is. The wealthier *campesino* may still sleep on it, though he will place it on a creaking brass bedframe. Tourists buy *petates* for use as yoga mats, sunbathing mats, picnic cloths, or even rugs.

The *petate* was not always a humble object. In pre-Conquest time it was used not only by the common people but by the rich and powerful as well. Treasures of jade, featherwork, fine textiles, gold, silver, and emeralds were kept in rolled *petates* and in *petate* chests. Moctezuma slept on a raised platform covered with a *petate* and he dined from platters of gold served on a reed mat.

Derived from the Aztec *petatl*, the *petate* has been used for centuries. Pre-Conquest codices depict its ancient use and even today it is still one of the most universally used objects that is made in the same way it always was, its patterns varying little throughout the country.

The tule *petate* is the most primitive type, but it is the specialty of the *petateros* of Ihuatzio who supply the needs of the surrounding population. Sr. Hernandez-Ramirez sells to people in the immediate area as well as to *revendadores*, or middlemen, who sometimes come from Mexico City and Morelia.

"Most I take to market in Pátzcuaro," said he. "I sell the small *petate* for two pesos, the large one, the *matrimonio* [the size of a double bed] for seven."

Friday is market day in Pátzcuaro and most of the craftsmen like Sr. Hernandez-Ramirez go to market by canoe (see Figure 3). The canoes, scooped-out logs, have been used for centuries on Lake

FIGURE 3

Pátzcuaro. Some of the towns on the lake's edge can be reached only by water. Early in the morning people from the islands and towns rimming the lake start coming into Pátzcuaro. They are warmly wrapped in *rebozos* and serapes for it is cold in this high country. Some have been rowing for two or three hours and once they dock, they must walk three kilometers into the center of town. Whole families— mothers, fathers, children, and grandparents—unload pottery, chickens, pigs, baskets, carved wood objects, copper utensils, vegetables, fruit, firewood, serapes, and textiles from their canoes. Most carry a large *petate* or two with them, either to sell or on which to display their wares.

We had been at the house of Sr. Hernandez-Ramirez all morning as he worked on his *petates*. As he added each reed, the *petate* grew diagonally. It took him an hour and a half to weave a small one and a whole day to make the large *matrimonio*. When he had finished, he showed us his mats on the rack on his porch. There were about twenty in all different sizes. As he spread them out to dry in the sun, they were various shades of green, pink-brown, mauve, and gold. As they dry, they turn solid gold, the color of the dried reed. Some of these *petates* would be taken to market the following Friday. Others are reserved for particular clients. Some would be held aside for the *revendadores* who might not come for weeks. A few, but very few, would be sold to tourists who might wander into the usually secluded region.

Working with the Craftsman

TOOLS AND MATERIALS

Tule (*Typhus Dominguensis*). The *petateros* gather two kinds of tule from Lake Pátzcuaro: *tule ancha* (called *chuspata*) and *tule redondo*, the round tule. Although the round tule is stronger and less of it is required to make a *petate*, the *chuspata* is more common. Neither type takes color, but those made from palm leaves will.

If the reeds are too dry, they will split, crack, or break and will not be flexible enough to work with. It is a good idea, therefore, to soak them all afternoon. After soaking the reeds, wait until the next day to work with them. Otherwise, they will be too soggy and bend too easily. Water may even spurt out while you are working.

A heavy stone or wooden mallet. If you use a stone, it must be smooth so that it does not tear the reed.

Sickle. The craftsman used a sickle, but a knife would work as well.

PROCEDURE

The basic *petate* designs used in Mexico are: the *cuadrado* (square weaving), the *jaspeado* (variegated weaving), and the *costilla* (the ribbed *petate*). The *costilla* which is the most common is described below:

1. Sr. Hernandez-Ramirez cracks about twenty tules in the center and places them near his working area (see Figure 10).

2. He always works with two tules at a time. Each one is bent in the center. Placing the flat sides together, the two reeds are placed one on top of the other. This procedure will make a softer *petate* that is "finished" on both sides. He picks up the reeds from the center fold, judging the placement of the reed from this center point so that it will be lined up correctly for the weaving. Hernandez-Ramirez now puts down the first pair of horizontal reeds (remember, one on top of the other, flat sides together).

3. Next another pair of reeds is inserted as a "V" around the first horizontal pair (Figures 4 and 5). At the point where the reed is bent, indent the inside of the reed with the thumbnail making a more definite crease; then bend the reed up. Now pound the intersection twice with quick but strong taps using the smooth stone. *This will be done each time a new weave is made.*

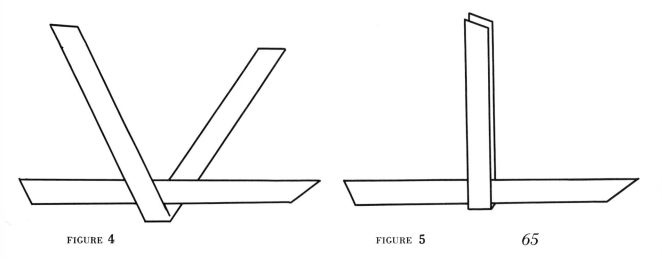

FIGURE 4   FIGURE 5   65

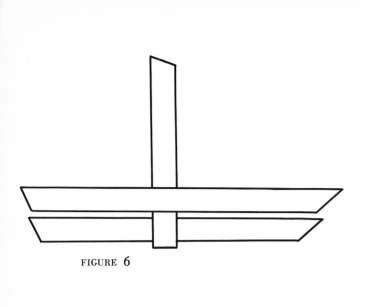

FIGURE **6**

FIGURE **7**

4. Now the craftsman takes up another pair of reeds. He keeps his foot on the reed intersection to hold the reeds in place when he reaches for more reed. If he has to leave the *petate* in progress, he places the stone over the working area. This third pair of reeds is laid over the vertical tules, above and contiguous to the horizontal reed (Figures 6 and 7). He pounds the reed with the stone.

5. Be sure to pick up both reeds (the pair) when you begin to weave. Don't leave the bottom reed laying there. Now he takes the lower right reed and folds it up sharply and tightly (Figure 8). He delineates the reed first with this thumbnail and pounds twice. (If at any time a reed breaks, weave in another immediately. You will need the correct number of reeds later so you won't lose count during the over-two, under-two weaving.)

*CRAFTS OF
MEXICO*

FIGURE **8**

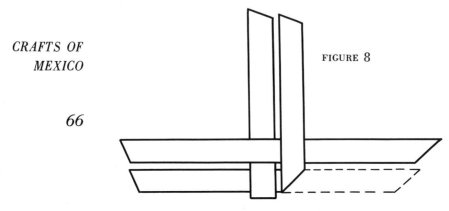

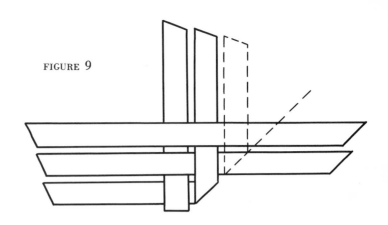

FIGURE 9

6. He takes another pair of reeds and lays them over the vertical reeds (Figure 9), remembering to keep his foot on each successive intersection.

7. He takes the lower right reed and folds it up again as in Step 5. There should always be one reed left after bending the horizontal reed up. This is how to tell where you are in the weaving.

8. Now—always from the right—Sr. Hernandez-Ramirez inserts the tule horizontally over two, under two, fold up bottom right, over two, under two, fold up bottom right and so on until he comes to the end (Figure 10). As each pair of reeds is woven in, there will of course be more to weave. Remember to pound the tule after each addition and keep the reed taut and woven closely together (Figure 11).

FIGURE 10

FIGURE 11

In the over-two, under-two pattern, be sure that you pick up the correct reeds and not part of another strand. It will be easier to recognize the correct reeds once you have woven in a few. The weaving itself, however, becomes more difficult as you have more reeds to weave in.

Remember to pick up the tule at the center in order to line it up. Then reach for the lower end, which will be your leading end. The tips of the tule are cut off later so don't worry about their condition. Weave through to the left, leading with the lower end. Always weave over two, under two. Remember to pound the newly woven area each time in order to flatten the reed.

It is easiest to work on the floor or on some other hard surface if you are working outside (not on the grass). And it will be easier to weave the *petate* if you keep your foot on it as you work.

As the woven portion increases, you may want to flatten the reed before you weave it in. The reed will become increasingly difficult to flatten as you weave more. A good heavy wooden mallet or a heavy, smooth stone is essential.

The *petate* will grow diagonally. Don't forget to fold up the lower right tule each time.

When Sr. Hernandez-Ramirez was about halfway through, his reed began to rustle and crackle. He was working in the sun and the reed had become too dry. He dipped the remaining reed in water for a minute or two. Then he began working again.

When the craftsman had woven 46 reeds into his *petate*, half of the mat was completed, yet all the necessary reeds had been inserted. To finish the other half, he proceeds as follows:

9. Nearing the end, he doubles over the reed and puts in the last reed. The usual end reed was left free.

10. Then he takes this free reed and weaves it back into the reeds that are already part of the mat. In this way, he begins to make the second half of the *petate* (Figure 12). The two following procedures are alternated and repeated over and over until all the reeds in this half of the *petate* are woven (Figure 13):

A. Take the end reed over 1, under 2, *over 3*, then under 2, over 2, under 2, and so on.

B. Take the next end reed over 1, under 2, *over 1*, then under 2, over 2, under 2, and so on.

Alternate these two procedures to form the other part of the *petate*. Be sure to continue to weave closely and to pound with a stone after each

weave.

FIGURE **12**

FIGURE **13**

11. Now weave in the edge of the other side of the *petate* exactly as explained in Step 10.

12. So far, Sr. Hernandez-Ramirez has been squatting. But now he sits on a low bench and extends his legs, holding the *petate* on his lap.

To finish the edge of the mat, he begins to braid the reed ends by putting the outer (first) reed over the second reed, then under the third (Figure 14). (The first reed is left laying over the mat and will be cut off later.) The second reed becomes the first reed, while

FIGURE 14

FIGURE 15

FIGURE 16

FIGURE **17**

FIGURE **18**

the third becomes the new second reed. Then the next reed is picked up and becomes the new third reed and these are braided (Figure 15). This process is repeated across the *petate*. At the end of this side, two reeds are left (Figure 16). The *petate* is turned over and these two reeds are braided into the new side in a continuous process (Figure 17). The weaver continues braiding (Figure 18) until he reaches the end. Then he inserts the ends into the *petate*.

PETATE

71

FIGURE 19

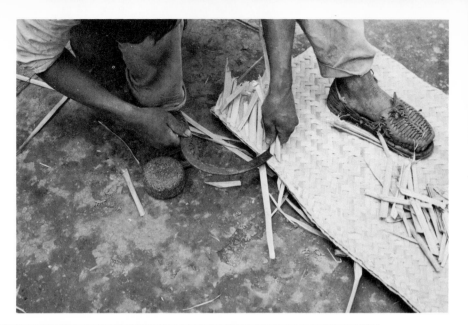

FIGURE 20

13. With the stone, he pounds along the braided edge, first on one side and then on the other.

14. With his sickle (the same sickle he uses to cut the tule at the lake), he cuts the remaining extra reeds (Figure 19). Sr. Hernandez-Ramirez is finished (Figure 20). It has taken him a little over an hour to make the *petate*.

CANASTO 5

Basketry is still one of the most important craft occupations in Mexico. With other reed weaving, it is one of Mexico's oldest crafts as well: it is thought to be older than pottery making and the weaving of textiles. Some of the forms and patterns are the same as they were before the Spanish came. Others are new. They have changed to meet the customers' demands particularly in Toluca and other areas near great metropolitan centers.

In each region of the country there are specialists: the towns of the basket weavers, the *petate* makers, and the sombrero makers exhibiting the distinct style of the region. Each uses the reed of his area. Those in Yucatán, for instance, weave fine products of *henequén*, others use *ixtle*. In the hot country, palm, bamboo, or sugar cane is used. In the high country, some may use the unwieldy willow as well as tule.

We had been told that Ihuatzio was the town of the basket weavers. Walking along the cobblestone streets of the peaceful little city, however, we saw only *petate* makers. It was only after we arrived in Ihuatzio that we were told we would find only a few. The *petatero*, Sr. Hernandez-Ramirez had told us who to see (see Chapter 4). On a narrow path bordered by tangled vines and low, flowering bushes we stopped to talk to a blind man. "Señor, can you tell us where we can find the house of

FIGURE 1

Agustín Pérez, the basket maker?" As the old man answered, he expertly scraped the heart of the *carrizo*, or bamboo, for the baskets.

Following his directions, we found the strong adobe house of Agustín Pérez. Nearby, the *carrizo* or bamboo stood in a narrow plot along one side of his land. Because this type of bamboo is not as readily available as the tule which grows wild in Lake Pátzcuaro, Agustín Pérez grows his own (Figure 1). To cut it he need only walk a few steps from his house. *Garucho*, which is what Sr. Pérez calls ordinary bamboo, can be used instead of the *carrizo*. "It is less flexible. It is strong, but it is harder to work with. The *garucho* comes from the low country. It is more expensive. Besides I have my own *carrizo* right here, why should I buy anything else?"

"I am a basket weaver. That is my main business," said Sr. Pérez. "But I raise chickens and I fish sometimes, too." Sr. Pérez makes the traditional basket of the region, the *chiquihuite*. Usually *chiquihuite* is the common term for different kinds of baskets, but here it means a basket made in one shape for general use. It is formed in many different sizes. Its form is distinct. Narrow at the bottom, flared slightly near the top, it is narrow at the top again. Sr. Pérez corrected us when we called the basket a "*canasta*." "This is a *canasto*," he said. "A basket without a handle. The *canasta* is a basket with a handle. I make the *chiquihuite*, the *canasto*, in all sizes—any size the customer wants." He also makes the mammoth basket hats in whose wide brims the bread deliverers of Mexico City carry *bolillos*, the popular Mexican hard rolls.

Some of Sr. Pérez's work is bought by the *revendadores* who sell his baskets in other parts of the country, Mexico City, Morelia, and perhaps Guadalajara. Only a few are sold in Ihuatzio. Some go to a regular clientel in Pátzcuaro, but he takes most of the baskets to market himself to sell at an average cost of three or four pesos.

In other areas of the country, large cone-shaped baskets serve as mini silos for the storage of grains and corn. Bird cages made of bamboo, sometimes five levels high, are covered with balconies, porticos, oriels, and spires. Furniture, houses, roofs, and even raincapes are made of reed. The ingenious *castillos*, the three-story-high frames for the fireworks used in the many fiestas of Mexico, are made of *carrizo* or bamboo. *Carrizo* is also used for *xuchiles*, the twenty-foot-tall armatures to which offerings of food or flowers are attached for various saints. Sr. Pérez, who can produce three baskets a day, limits himself to the basket forms of his region. His simple *canasto*, the traditional basket form of Ihuatzio, is the most beautiful of all (see Plates 4 and 5).

Working with the Craftsman

The *canasto* model made by Sr. Pérez (Figure 2) is 10 inches high with a 42-inch circumference at the top and a 36½-inch circumference at

FIGURE 2

the bottom. The widest circumference, three-quarters of the way up the basket, is 45 inches. All of these measurements are outside dimensions. The diameter of the top is just a little wider than the height of the basket. Its sides flow gently outward from the base, reaching their greatest flare two inches from the top.

The main framework of the basket contains 9 staves, each 44 inches in length. There are about 23 woven reeds in the bottom of the *canasto*, the diameter of which is 11 inches. The sides contain about 61 rows of reed or 8 inches, and 12 rows of the stronger top weave. The bound rim is 1 inch high and contains about 5 or 6 woven reeds. These measurements need not be followed exactly, but they give an idea of the number of reeds you may need to use for each part of the basket.

TOOLS AND MATERIALS

Carrizo. A form of bamboo that is more pliable, but not as strong as ordinary bamboo. Split bamboo can also be used, but it is harder to work with. The reed is usually 7 or 8 feet tall. Agustín Pérez cuts it into workable lengths as he uses it.
A slate.
A stone.
A knife.

PREPARATION OF MATERIALS

Agustín Pérez spends two or three days cutting and preparing the *carrizo.* "I can cut the *carrizo* all year, but I cut it only as I need it. It can be used a year after it is planted. There is a wild stand near here, but that is all besides mine. There are not many basket makers in Ihuatzio." Sr. Pérez uses the same knife for cutting the *carrizo* as he does for the basketry. I asked him how he kept his knife sharp. "I don't," he answered. "When you come from the States again, will you bring me another one?"

After splitting the thin reed, he cuts each half once more (Figure 3) making 4 reeds. The underside is scraped clean with a knife and the spines or joints (*espinas*) are cut down. After being split once, the reed is gently cracked at each joint or spine so it will not split or break later.

FIGURE 3

FIGURE 4

To make the staves or *barras*, Sr. Pérez uses a smooth rounded stone to pound half the stalk on a flat stone or slate (Figure 4); in doing so, the meat and the spines of the *carrizo* are broken down further. The *cáscara* or the shell of the *carrizo* is used for the binding edge. To prepare it, the meat is scraped clean from the shell thus making it much more flexible. In the preparation of the materials for the *canasto*, the meat of the reed is only left on the staves to provide added strength. Here was the only instance of waste we found in our craft travels. Sr. Pérez said he could think of no way to use this scraped center of the *carrizo*. After the reeds have been cut and scraped, they must be soaked all afternoon on the day before they are used. This makes them pliant and workable.

PROCEDURE

1. Agustín Pérez trims the ends of the staves and cuts them squarely as he prepares to lay out the bottom of the basket.

CANASTO

77

2. After positioning two staves at right angles, exterior side up on a flat stone or slate, he places the other 7 staves one atop the other like the spokes of a wheel, centering each stave (Figure 5). He keeps his foot on the intersection of the staves so that their placement will not be disturbed. If he is called away, he uses the round stone to secure his work. The staves, the stone, and the reeds are kept where they can be reached easily without moving his foot.

3. The reeds are usually woven two at a time, but it is a good idea to start with just one. Agustín Pérez began about 3 inches from the center of the stave configuration, weaving over and under the staves (Figure 6).

4. After the first reed is woven around 4 or 5 staves, he tucks the second reed under the first one. Then with both hands, first working one and then the other, he alternately weaves the reeds one above the stave, the other beneath. This double weaving holds the staves securely (Figure 7).

FIGURE 5

FIGURE 6   FIGURE 7

5. Still holding the staves with his foot, Agustín pivots slowly as he weaves the base of the *canasto*. (Remember to use both reeds, one after the other, by weaving around 4 or 5 staves at a time, then going back to pick up the other reed. Keep the woven reed taut and weave closely.) If at any time your reed becomes dry and unwieldy or begins to break, dampen or wet it.

6. When Agustín Pérez reaches the end of a reed, he clips the end and pokes it down through the already-woven reeds. A new reed is begun in the same manner except it is inserted one stave back (Figure 8). He also clips the end of each new reed as he begins to use it. If a reed breaks, just take a new reed, go back one stave, and continue.

CANASTO

79

FIGURE 8

7. After weaving 9 or 10 rows or reed, turn the *canasto* base over. From now on, you will be raising the sides. The top or exterior side of the *carrizo* which until now has been face up, will now be face down: the bottom of the basket.

8. Taking one stave at a time, Agustín Pérez bends each toward the inside of the basket. He supports the underside of the stave with his left forefinger and the forefingers of his other hand as he places both thumbs against the outside. He presses the stave forward slowly and carefully so it will not crack. If it does crack, continue. The subsequent weaving will still hold it in place unless it is a complete break. This is one of the reasons it is vital to soak all the reeds well before using them.

Moving his right hand halfway up the stave and keeping his left hand where it was, he bends the stave more (Figure 9). This takes a great deal of strength.

9. Transferring the *canasto* to his lap, Agustín sits on a low stool and begins to weave with two reeds again as he did in Steps 3 and 4 (Figure 10). As you weave, press in on the staves with a great deal of pressure so the staves will not "fall out."

10. Agustín Pérez continues to mold and press the staves as he weaves. When raising the sides, he does not insert the ends of the reeds as he did for the base. He merely terminates the reed (by cutting if necessary), making it end on the inside of the basket halfway across a stave where it is held in place by pressure (see Figure 15). For a new reed, begin it the same way, one stave back.

11. About 8 inches up the sides (55 reeds up) the staves are bent toward the inside of the basket (Figure 11). Bend according to the directions in Step 8.

12. Now the *canasto* begins to curve in. This will be approximately the last quarter of the basket. To provide more inward pressure and to cinch in the top of the basket, change the weaving pattern—weave over two staves, under one (Figure 12). Continue weaving with two reeds. Mold and press in the staves as you weave. Weave about 10 rows.

13. About 1 inch of each stave should now be exposed; if there is more, cut it off with a straight cut. With a sharp knife, Agustín Pérez scores the inside edge of each stave where it meets the horizontal reeds and bends each forward (Figure 13).

14. Scrape the meat from the underside of the exposed stave, leaving only the *cáscara* or outer shell of the *carrizo*. Then with the

FIGURE 9

FIGURE 10

FIGURE 11

FIGURE 12

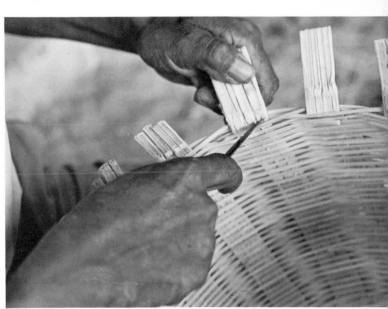

FIGURE 13

CANASTO

81

FIGURE 14

FIGURE 15

FIGURE 16

FIGURE 17

help of a knife, insert the stave shell into the second or third weave from the top of the *canasto* (Figure 14).

15. Agustín prepares two long *cáscaras* (in the same way he did the staves at the top of the basket) by scraping the meat from the length of 2 reeds. The *cáscaras* are slightly green, but being newly cut, they are more flexible. He wets them and, with his knife, he pushes the two *cáscaras* between the fifth and sixth reeds down beginning to wind them around the rim of the basket to form the binding edge. One *cáscara* starts from the outside of the *canasto*, the other from the inside (Figures 15 and 16). Inserting the ends with his knife, he pulls the *cáscara* through while still holding the other end. He alternately loops each one, one following the other, so that the whole rim is bound. He places the tip of the *cáscara* into the next insertion point to get it out of the way while he pulls through the previous part of the *cáscara*. Keep the *cáscara* taut and woven closely together.

16. When he comes to the end, Agustín makes a space with the knife about six reeds down from the *cáscara* binding. He puts the end through this, bends it up, and cuts off the rest (Figure 17).

17. The *canasto* is completed. Agustín simply checks it over and breaks off any free reeds he finds. It has taken him one hour to weave it.

6 CORAZÓN DE TRIGO

In Tzintzuntzan, the Place of the Hummingbirds, graceful figures of wheat are woven. Birds, stars, angels, virgins, musicians, soldiers, animals, and velocipedes are all painstakingly handcrafted from the stalk of the wheat, a product that came with the Spanish.

Once the capital of the powerful Tarascan empire, Tzintzuntzan is now a small village located below the ruins of the *yacatas,* the low, blunt, pre-Conquest pyramids destroyed long ago by the conquerors. Some of the streets and even the church are built with stones taken from the debris of the destroyed *yacatas.* This town is the home of Plácido Pablo (Figure 1). Known as the weaver of all the Christs of Tzintzuntzan, he was the first to weave fanciful figures from the *paja de trigo.*

The weaving of tule and sometimes palm figures has long been done near Toluca. These figures are larger and more durable than those of *trigo* (wheat) and the result is entirely different. The weaving of palms for Palm Sunday is traditional in Mexico. We have seen plaited, twisted, fluted, and frilled *palmas* of bizarre shapes woven for the competitions between the palm weavers. The *corazón* is a ritual object, too, but its philosophy dates back farther in Mexico than that of Palm Sunday which came with the Spanish. No one could really say how long it has been used.

84

FIGURE 1

It is not until one passes behind the roadside stands, under the twisted 400-year-old olive trees, and beyond a sixteenth century monastery that one really enters the town of Tzintzuntzan. We stepped through a side gate onto a cobbled street never touched by cars. The street shortly turns into a path. After crossing a ravine and going up a short hill, we came to the house of Plácido Pablo. The Pablos live simply. Because they are not landowners, they work only with the reed. They were the only craftsmen we visited who had no chairs. Tree stumps were brought from the house and covered with newspapers for us.

Passersby greeted Sr. Pablo as *Tata*, a term of affection and respect in this part of the country. It refers to the Spaniard, Don Vasco de Quiroga, a tireless and good man who, centuries ago, organized the villagers around the lake into guilds, created new crafts, and revived old ones.

Tata Plácido, whose father and grandfather made the simple *petates* before him, is known primarily for his figures of Christ (see Figure 2). He has difficulty making them now because of rheumatism in his hands. His wife and his youngest son help him. He calls Sra. Pablo, *Castellana*, because her principal language is Spanish. Tarasco is still spoken in Michoacán. For many it is their only language.

FIGURE 2

Sra. Pablo knelt on the dirt floor of the house grinding wheat on the *metate*, the grinding stone and pestle of volcanic ash. The stalks would be used for the *figuras*, but the grain would be eaten. Nothing here is wasted. The grain is saved only for the *corazón* because is is part of the design.

In his mellifluous, singsong voice Tata Plácido told us how he began making the *figuras*. "Years ago, when I was a young man, I went before the Virgin and I said, 'Why can't I, a poor Indian, with these rough hands, who can't read or write, make something beautiful?' Soon after, I was hurt in a fight. I could not work sitting up. I had to lay down for many weeks. I could not make the *petates*. An American came to me and asked me to make a dog of tule. I did. I also made a chicken. He paid me well—14 centavos. But then, what—fifty-five years ago? That was a lot of money. I began to make more *figuras*. Then I thought of the wheat. It would be easier to use, it is more flexible. I could make more things." When asked how he got his ideas, Tata Pablo replied, *"Me revelaba*: I dream them." His ideas come from pictures, too. He showed us a yellowed newspaper with a picture of a velocipede.

Once he had begun making *figuras*, Tata Plácido never made a *petate* again. For several years he was an unpaid teacher of *figura* weaving in the school of Tzintzuntzan. To do this he first had to learn Spanish. Then with the help of a cultural mission, which no longer exists, he taught weaving in all the schools around the lake and in Morelia, too. For this he received an hourly wage. He told us it takes three months to learn this work. Some of his disciples have become well known. One weaves great Christs on the Cross that are twelve to fifteen feet high. Another, Don Pedro Silva of Ihuatzio, has exhibited his work throughout the world, although he too still lives simply.

The weaving of reed is difficult. We went back three times to find a reed figure that could be easily explained. The *soplador* or fan which is the basis for an angel I had proposed to do was much too intricate. Finally, Plácido, Jr. made the *corazón de trigo* (Figure 3 and Plate 5), a ritual object that is sometimes put in the fields or the house to ask for a good crop or more food. It is also used as a fertility symbol. However, some say it is just for good luck.

FIGURE 3

CORAZÓN DE TRIGO

87

The family worked together: Plácido, Jr. worked in the small area before the door of the house, his mother cleaned the wheat stalks and stripped them of their dried leaves, and Tata Plácido wove a delicate lampshade of *paja* over a tree stump. As they wove, Tata Plácido talked. He spoke in Spanish although when the Pablos talked among themselves they spoke Tarasco, the ancient language of the region.

"This reed is good," he said, adding another to the delicate *lámpara*. "I try to buy all my wheat at once, just after the harvest. Enough to last all year. If I don't have enough, I have to buy the *monojas*. They are 8 pesos. It is too expensive." He showed us where he stored the *trigo* in the rafters of his house beneath the tile roof.

The reed weavers are possibly the poorest paid of the craftsmen. Sometimes they have no orders. All say that what they need is a decent market for their products. In the Pátzcuaro market I bought a three-handled *soplador* for 1 peso. As I turned to leave, the *vendedora* called me back. It was not one *soplador* for 1 peso, but two. She gave me another. This amounted to a half peso an hour for her work. The small flat reed figures made by Tata Plácido are only 2 pesos. The prices rise as the *figuras* become larger, but they are still too inexpensive.

Back in the market *puestos* along the road to Pátzcuaro, we walked through the stands. Here, along with the fine earthenware pots and dishes, we saw every kind of reed figure made: Christs of the Cross, intricate churches, church scenes, bandstands with reed musicians, a stagecoach, lacelike lampshades, ferris wheels, merry-go-rounds, large reed planes and trains, angels of all sizes, little birds, and large birds, animals, and velocipedes. All had been begun by Tata Plácido, the innovator of a new art form.

Working with the Craftsman

TOOLS AND MATERIALS

A bundle of wheat. 50 to 70 stalks. Choose wheat with healthy golden grain for this is much of the design.

A bowl of water to dampen the wheat if it becomes dry and starts to split.

Twine.

Scissors.

PROCEDURE

1. Plácido, Jr. begins by holding 2 stalks (Figure 4) parallel to one another. You will always work with 2 stalks at a time. Line up the grain tips (the ends containing the wheat kernels) so they are even.

2. Take 2 more stalks (B) with grain tips aligned and cross over stalks A about 2 inches from the top (Figure 4).

3. Holding crossed stalks A and B in one hand, take 2 more stalks (C) and place them over B parallel to A (Figure 5).

4. Bend C down, back, and under B (Figure 6). Still holding all the stalks, take the end of stalk C and bend it up over C and A, parallel to B (Figure 7). At this point, your stalks will look like Figure 8: 2 grain tips and 2 stalk ends on the left, 4 grain tips on the right, and 2 stalks on each lower side.

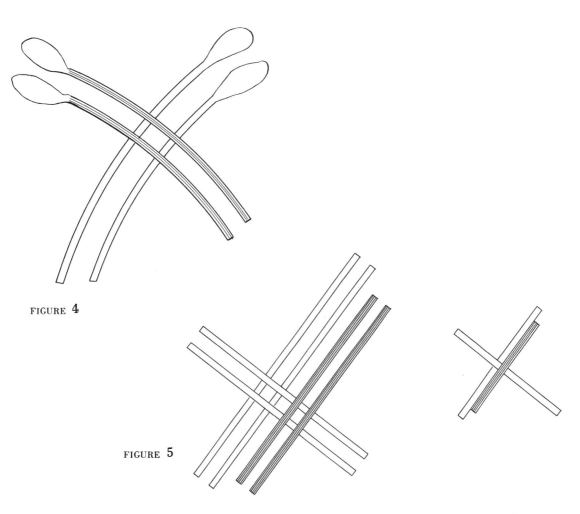

FIGURE 4

FIGURE 5

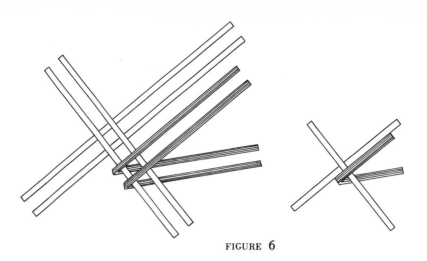

FIGURE 6

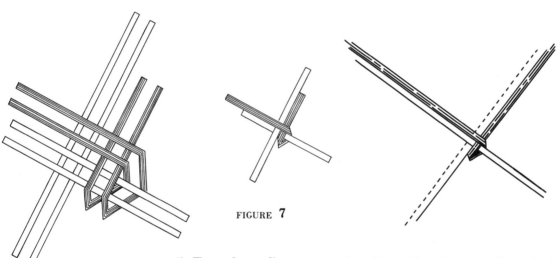

FIGURE 7

5. Turn the stalks over so the side with 2 loose stalk ends is at the right. Try not to disturb the placement of the stalks. The right side will now have the 2 grain tips; the left will have 4 grain tips, the opposite of Figure 8.

6. Now take 2 more stalks (D). Align them with the 2 grain tips on the right, crossing over the other stalks but parallel to those on the right (Figure 9).

7. Fold the ends of D down and under the crossed stalks as in Figure 6, then up and to the left over the other stalks as in Figure 7. Keep the wheat taut. Make well-creased, sharp, tight folds so the weave will not be loose. Place the stalks closely together.

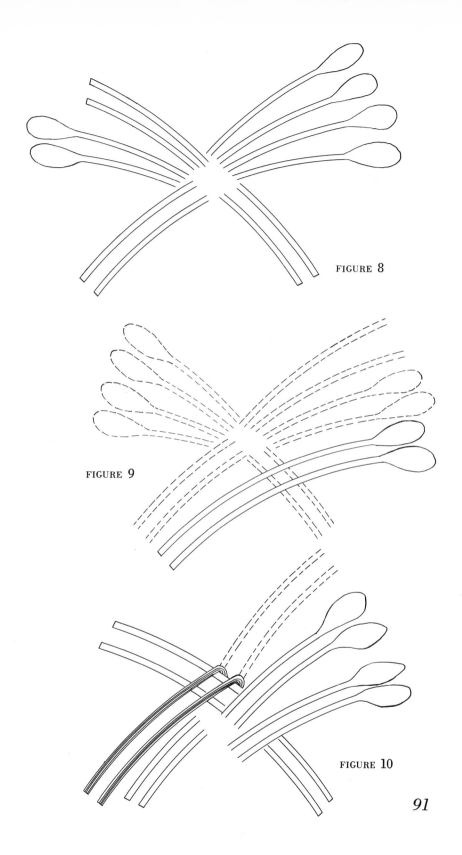

FIGURE 8

FIGURE 9

FIGURE 10

91

8. Now the 2 loose ends at the right are bent down over the loose-ended stalk D and pressed parallel to Y (Figure 10).

9. Turn over to the other side. Repeat the process. Add stalks E the same way as stalks D and continue. You will use approximately 60 stalks. Follow Figures 9, 5, 7, and 10 and then turn over and begin again. The loose ends are always on the right when you add the new stalks. Remember to keep the stalks firm, especially when bending. After you have added several pairs of stalks, you will begin to see a pattern (Figure 11).

If your wheat begins to split or break, dampen the unused wheat or put it in water for a minute or so.

10. The size of the *corazón* is usually determined by the length of the wheat. You are at the end whenever your stalks extend only far enough beyond the apex to be secured at the bottom of the *corazón* or whenever the mass becomes too bulky for your hand to hold—whichever comes first. Pull the last 2 stalks on the outer right to cinch in. The ends are then tucked in (Figure 12). Snip off any ends left over on these 2 stalks.

FIGURE 11

FIGURE 12

FIGURE 13

FIGURE 14

FIGURE 15

11. Take 4 stalks from each inner side of the bottom of the *corazón* and pull together firmly (Figure 13). If you wish, you may braid each of these 4 stalks into a strand. Plácido, Jr. did not. If you do, gently flatten the stalks with a stone, mallet or other object before you plait (I used a Coke bottle). It will make the wheat smoother and easier to work. When the plaiting is completed, tie the 2 ends together and trim about 1 inch below the knot (Figure 14).

12. If you do not braid, merely tie the two ends together with a twine slip knot, pulling the stalks taut (Figure 15).

CORAZÓN DE TRIGO

93

FIGURE **16**

FIGURE **17**

13. Clip the wheat below the tied area to about 1 inch.

14. Clip the lower stalk ends upward and inward slightly so they are more or less even (Figure 16). If you wish, you may clip a small amount from the tops of the wheat cilia.

15. Pound the woven area gently to flatten the weave (Figure 17). This is a fun craft that is easy to do, once you get started. When we wove our own *corazones* along with Plácido, Jr., who was teaching us, we became so fascinated that we realized we were forgetting to take notes and photographs. My first endeavor was rough and loosely woven. Be sure to make tight corners and to keep the wheat taut at all times in order to produce a craftsmanlike *corazón* for luck or decoration.

METALS

FISH OF SILVER 7

The old city of Pátzcuaro which stands above Mexico's most beautiful lake, Lake Pátzcuaro, looks like no other place in Mexico. Since 1324 it has presided over this lakeland domain in indulgent serentity. Its massive buildings with heavy, carved wooden beams and overhung orange tiled roofs make Pátzcuaro look very much like Medieval Spain.

The *pescado blanco*, or white fish, which inhabit the lake have always been the economic backbone of the city. Even in pre-Conquest days, it was considered as much a delicacy as it is today. But if Moctezuma savored these fish, they were probably not from this lake for the Tarascan empire of which Pátzcuaro was a part was one of the few regions that successfully rebuffed the aggressive Aztecs and remained independent.

Symbols of the Pátzcuaro waters—the lake itself, the fish, the islands, the boats, the nets, the ducks, the reeds—have all been subjects of Pátzcuaro arts. Recessed in the thick stone walls of the village churches surrounding the lake are *cantera* (limestone) plaques of fishing scenes. Pottery of the region is decorated with naïve sketches of fishermen, thier nets, the lake reed, the ducks, and the fish.

The cultural life of Pátzcuaro is also closely allied with these symbols. At fiestas, dancers hold six-foot papier-mâché *pescados blancos* on their shoulders during the Dance of the Fish. Others, for the Dance of the Butterflies, bear fish headdresses and gracefully scooped butterfly nets. To celebrate the Day of Our Lady of Salud, the atrium of the Basilica is festooned with immense fishing nets and chanting fishermen parade before the saint, their nets held high. Outside on floats, fishermen raise offerings of *pescado blanco* to a facsimile of the Virgen de la Salud (see Chapter 13). The lake is even the principal element in the Spanish coat-of-arms of Pátzcuaro.

On market day in Pátzcuaro one still can see women from the lake villages wearing necklaces of the fish of silver of centuries ago (Plate 6), for the Pátzcuaro silversmith continues to make this classic jewelry so intimately connected with the history and the daily life of the region.

The Cazares, a mestizo family, have been silver- and goldsmiths for several generations although in the beginning they made only religious objects.

After the Conquest, the Spanish decreed the natives could not work with silver or other fine metals. Silver- and goldsmithing became a Spanish and then a mestizo art. By the time the law was repealed, the family traditions were set. Few Indian jewelers are found in Mexico today.

The Spanish had almost immediately wiped out the fine workmanship previously attained in pre-Conquest Mexico. They rejected the fusing of gold and silver, the intricate mosaic work, the jointed fish, the complicated animals, and the flowers and bells. The platters, bowls, vases, and jewelry made by hammering, lost wax, repoussée, cloisonée, or mold techniques were all discarded. This dazzling work was melted into bullion and sent to Spain. Now the precious metals were used extravagantly for the new religion, the Christianity of the Spanish. Churches boasted altars of solid silver; whole walls and ceilings were encrusted with thick gold leaf. The myriad saints were bedecked in robes embedded with emeralds and pearls. What was not used for the church was sent to Spain. The pre-Conquest methods were not used again until the 1930's when the lagging silver industry was put on a new course.

But Pátzcuaro was to stay out of this mainstream. Away from the direct center of Spanish civilization, the old designs were never really lost; they continued to be made. During the revolutions the mining of silver ceased, but when the work began again, Pátzcuaro went back to its old ways.

Today Mexico leads the world in the export of silver. But this makes little difference to a family such as the Cazares, the conservator of Pátzcuaro's traditional jewelry. A mestizo family, the Cazares have been silver and goldsmiths for several generations.

The Cazares family was originally from Uruapan (see Chapter 14), a semi-tropical city a few kilometers from Pátzcuaro. During the Revolution of 1910, however, Herminio Cazares was forced to flee his native town and in 1913 he settled in Pátzcuaro, where his son Jesus was born.

Taking up silver work again, Herminio began by making *arracadas*, the large hooped earrings of the lake country. He found that the people of Pátzcuaro were making the fish of silver and he improved on their workmanship and design thus helping to revive this art. He also began once more to make religious objects for the church: small, finely-wrought crowns, rosaries, halos, and crosses—even miniature gold slippers. He made the golden *custodia* (the elaborate metal holder for the host), for one of the main Pátzcuaro churches, and also the town's golden Virgen de la Salud, censers, fonts, and other sacred plates, vessels, and altar decorations. "But when the Indians made saints for the churches," said Jesus Cazares, "they made them hollow, putting their idols inside."

Two of Mexico's most prominent artists have designed jewelry for Pátzcuaro. Robert Montenegro formed a pin of a man and a woman sitting in a little silver boat, the hollowed log *canoa* of Pátzcuaro. After visiting the lakeside *pueblo* of Ihuatzio (see Chapters 4 and 5), Miguel Covarrubias sketched a man and woman in a canoe below which hung four, fat fish. He offered Herminio Cazares the sketch from which to make a piece of jewelry. Herminio was busy and put the sketch in a drawer, but his son, Jesus, who was still a boy when Covarrubias came, liked the design and that night he took it out of the drawer and made a lead model of a brooch. After seeing the model, Herminio was persuaded and formed the pin in silver. It has since become a classic. We first saw the Covarrubias pin in the Museo de Artes Populares in Mexico City where Jesus now displays examples of the classic jewelry of Pátzcuaro.

In the Cazares workshop, Jesus showed us a necklace called the *boda*. This wedding necklace was used before the Spanish came. The women here always wore the coral beads and the metal *cascabeles*, but slowly the idea of Christianity was worked into the necklace and it became a large rosary.

Before this a suitor in the lake villages would take the necklace to the father of the girl he wanted to marry. If the father accepted him as a future son-in-law, he then offered the necklace to his daughter. If she accepted the admirer, she kept the necklace; if she refused him, the father returned it.

"This is no longer done," said Jesus. "But still—in the country —most brides wear the *boda* necklace during the wedding ceremony. It is her wedding gift—so many are still made."

Sr. Cazares showed us how he made the filigreed *cascabeles*. They are formed of flat silver tracery in such a way that when folded up and soldered, they create a globe. At the same time, he was making his daughter a *boda* of coral from Veracruz. "The real coral is seldom used now," he said. "It is too expensive and difficult to get." The Cazares began using Czechoslovakian *porcelana* in 1922. Once 2.50 pesos a kilo, it is now 300 pesos. Sr. Cazares believes these dark orange-red porcelain beads are no longer made, although they are available from a company in Mexico City that bought up huge stocks several years ago when the prices began to go up. "Tarascan metallurgy was highly developed in pre-Spanish Mexico," said Sr. Cazares. "The fish and the *cascabeles* were made of copper as well as silver then. The *cascabeles* had tiny stones, bones, or clay inside so they would make a noise when worn. The women always wore the beads of coral. Then, the wealthy wore silver; the poor, copper."

The jointed fish made of very thin silver is a traditional art form in Pátzcuaro as well. "I still make some *milagros*," Sr. Cazares told us. "Many fish *milagros* are made here for fishermen wanting to give thanks for a good catch. Yes, you can see many *milagros* here in the churches."

Jesus Cazares also told us of another kind of fish ornament that was made by his father, Herminio. These were large silver fish for the costumes used in the Dance of the Christians and the Moors in Ihuatzio. (This is a traditional conflict dance, reliving the historical battle in Spain between the Christians and the Moors. It is still danced in Ihuatzio as well as in other towns on the Day of St. Francis.) We saw these ancient costumes at the house of Luciana Jerónimo in Ihuatzio. Fish of silver like the small ones on the necklaces, but four inches long, were suspended from heads of silver lions and silver eagles. Small fish dangled from a cornucopia and other fish of silver clasped the chap-like pants of the Christians' costumes. These silver ornaments jangle when the revelers dance, adding to the staccato rhythm of the music.

"The silver for these costumes cost 1000 pesos in my father's day. I have not made any for years. But recently I received an order."

A woman entered the *taller* as Sr. Cazares was talking. She was wrapped in a faded *rebozo* of the region. Her hair hung down her back in one thick braid entwined with red yarn. "How much will you pay for these *arracadas*?" she asked. The *arracadas* are the varied, crescent-shaped hooped earrings of the region. These were fine, heavy antiques. Once, each village had its distinct style. He looked them over and tested them. "Five hundred pesos," he said.

"Not enough," she said indignantly and left.

Sometimes Sr. Cazares will buy old silver and old coins, those old enough to contain the required amount of silver. Mexican sterling is 900 parts pure silver to 100 parts copper rather than the 925 to 75 ratio that is common to the United States. But Sr. Cazares buys most of his silver in ingots from the bank in Morelia where the quality is controlled by the government.

The woman trying to sell her antique earrings was part of Jesus Cazares' long-standing clientel which includes those from the city who may buy more modern ware, and those from the lake villages whose needs are bound by custom. Other jewelers buy his traditional jewelry and some sell it at a 100 percent mark-up. The two necklaces, the fish of silver and the *boda* had cost only 300 pesos. I asked him why he didn't raise his prices.

"I have been thinking of it," he said.

Working with the Craftsman

This project is best suited to the jewelry worker who already has tools, equipment, and experience with metals. The fish of silver would be an extremely difficult "first" project.

Sr. Cazares painstakingly chisels and finish forms the fish by hand until they are really works of art. For this reason, other silversmiths in Pátzcuaro may tell you they are Cazares—they know he is the best.

TOOLS AND MATERIALS

Male and female bronze ring molds.

Dry cement mixed with automobile transmission oil.

4 fish molds. They can be made of clay although those used by **Sr.**

Cazares were made of silver which is more durable. (Sr. Cazares has cast his own fish and ring molds.)

A 3-inch thick block of *wood* and 2 thinner "sandwiches" (see Figure 7) of wood

Charcoal, a flat piece about 3 inches in diameter.

A regular file and a set of graduated files, from fine to finer, both rounded and 3-sided.

A jackknife.

A magnet.

A small crucible and long-handled tongs.

A wooden stick.

A long metal blowpipe.

Borax.

A pan of water.

Round nose pliers.

Steel polishers.

Emery paper of graduated fineness.

A hand clamp.

A graver.

A small lead tablet and a piece of paper.

A small, round-headed hammer (ball peen hammer).

Three stamps, one for the eye of the fish, one for the pupil of the eye, and one for the scales.

A knob-handled knife with a tip like that of a mat-cutting knife.

A soldering iron.

A kerosene lamp for soldering if you do not use an electric soldering iron.

Sulfuric or muriatic acid or, *tempered clay cup, water, salt and lemon juice.*

Detergent.

A handkerchief.

Smooth stone or *diamond dust.*

69 coral stones or *porcelain "coral."*

Silver wire for chain. It is suggested that you buy wire instead of trying to make it yourself although this can be done. (You will need of course, a forge, bellows and fuel. Sr. Cazares used charcoal and started the fire with kerosene.)

PROCEDURE

1. Sr. Cazares places four fish molds near one another on his working area. His molds are silver, but they could be made of clay. They are replicas of the Pátzcuaro white fish, 1 inch long and a fraction over $\frac{1}{4}$ inch at the widest fin-spread.

2. Taking one bronze ring mold which has a funnel through which to pour the molten silver, he places it over the four fish (Figure 1).

3. With his hand he heaps the damp mixture into the ring mold and presses it over the fish (Figure 2). He tamps it down hard and levels it with a block of wood. (This cement is mixed with regular automobile transmission oil giving it a consistency much like wet sand, but more cohesive. Add only enough oil to mold the cement easily.)

FIGURE 1   FIGURE 2

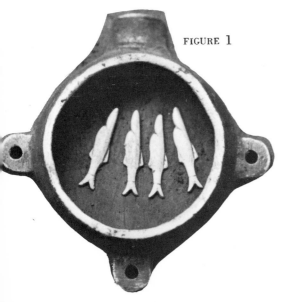

Natural limestone of this region, crushed and strained through fine mesh, was once used for this mixture. *Piloncillo*, a low quality brown sugar was dissolved in water and used as its cohesive agent. (*Piloncillo*, sold in cone shapes in the market, is usually used in cooking.) The mixture had to be dried before using it or the sugar would explode when the liquid silver was poured into the mold. This limestone mixture was used until about 1945 when cars began to appear in greater number in Pátzcuaro—and with them, transmission oil.

4. When the contemporary cement blend is well tamped into the mold, Sr. Cazares turns the mold over. The fish prototypes are at the surface half embedded in the mixture. This is one half of the mold.

5. With a jackknife, he gently cuts the *jitos* or channels from the tips of the noses of the fish down to the lip of the ring mold (Figures 3 and 5). He then cleans off the extra cement.

6. He files charcoal onto the surface of the mold until it is well covered so that the two molds will not stick together when joined.

7. Next he places the second ring mold on top of the first. The prototypes are on the surface of the bottom mold now; the bottom of the second mold will make the other half of the impression.

8. He applies the cement mixture as in Step 3, tamping it and leveling it with the block of wood.

9. Separating the ring mold, he puts the top half aside right side up. (Figure 4).

FIGURE 3

FIGURE 4

FIGURE 5

FIGURE 6

10. With the jackknife, he loosens the prototypes in the bottom mold and turns it over so the fish drop out.

11. On the second mold, he cuts the channels as in Step 5 (Figure 5).

12. Sr. Cazares uses a primitive forge: a small open brick oven. He starts a charcoal fire with kerosene and for bellows he uses a hand-turned wheel that causes air to go from a box through a tube to the fire (Figure 6). The handle of the wheel is secured with baling wire. Because the fire must be hot, it takes a half hour of almost continuous turning of the wheel to force enough air into the fire to bring it to the necessary temperature. He begins the fire at this point in his work.

FISH OF SILVER

13. He sets his crucible in a niche in the side of the oven. The clay crucible must be heated gradually so it will not crack. (There are commercial crucibles that can stand great heat. In Mexico, a bone alloy is sometimes used.) Sr. Cazares had his crucible made of clay in Tzintzuntzan.

While waiting for the fire to get hot and the crucible to warm, Sr. Cazares gathers the scraps of silver filings he has collected on a piece of paper and puts them in a drawer under his work area. To this he adds a couple of silver coins (old enough to be sterling), and an old fish of silver. This is some of the silver used in the model. (There are twelve fish on the model.)

14. Lifting the warmed crucible with tongs, he puts this silver into it and then places the crucible right into the fire. (Silver melts at 1781° F. or 960° C.) While the silver is melting, Sr. Cazares works the wheel and fans the fire with a *soplador*, a reed fan, to increase the temperature.

15. With a wooden stick held by tongs, he removes the larger pieces of charcoal that have fallen into the silver from the fire; the remainder burn out. Then with a long metal blowpipe, he blows out more of the carbon in the silver.

16. He picks up the connected ring molds between wooden "sandwich" blocks so he will not burn his hands when the silver is poured (Figure 7).

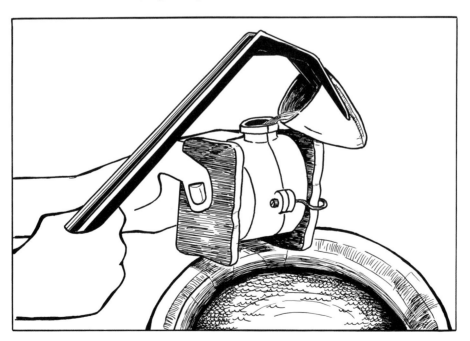

FIGURE 7

FIGURE 8

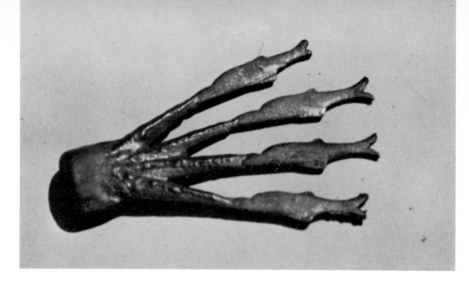

17. Holding the ring mold in one hand, he puts a pinch of borax onto the surface of the molten silver. It acts as a flux and helps to prevent oxidation of the metal. The borax keeps the silver fluid for the instant it takes to pour it into the mold.

18. With tongs, he lifts the crucible and pours the red-hot silver into the lip of the mold (Figure 7). (It had cooled so fast that part of one fish's tail broke off. The molten silver must be poured very quickly.)

This method of pouring seems extremely precarious: the silver is red-hot and the pourer could miss. But safety practices are almost nonexistent in Mexico. Small children often wander around the most dangerous work areas. Yet, I have never seen anyone hurt.

19. Sr. Cazares opens the mold quickly and tosses the fish of silver into a pan of water (Figure 8).

20. While the fish were cooling, Sr. Cazares showed us how he makes silver *alambre* (wire) for the necklaces. For this, too, is made by hand.

In a clay mold, he pours a bar of silver a little smaller than a large candy bar. Removing the ingot from the mold, he pounds it with an iron mallet on an anvil which is secured to the top of a waist-high tree stump. He pounds along the side of the bar until a small flat piece has "grown" along the edge. This distended portion is then cut and the next flank is pounded. It takes two hours of constant pounding to flatten the solid bar.

He now pulls the wire through the *hilero,* a metal bar with holes of graduated sizes. This is done by means of a makeshift pulley with heavy, hook-handled pliers attached to one end for securing the rope; the silver wire, attached to the other end of the rope, is drawn through successively smaller holes of the *hilero* until it is the desired size.

FIGURE 9

21. Returning to the fish, Sr. Cazares now uses pliers to cut off the sprue, the silver that has hardened in the *jitos* (Figure 9).

22. With a series of files, emery paper, and steel polishers, he now takes each fish separately, puts it in a hand clamp, and perfects its form. "The mold is always imperfect," explains Sr. Cazares. The finishing is done on both sides. There are many poor examples of fish of silver to be found around Pátzcuaro which are barely more than mold-poured and are often formed only on one side, or in half molds. Sr. Cazares makes his fish of silver in the old, painstaking way.

The next several steps, which include incising, delineating, filing, smoothing, finishing, and polishing are repeated procedures. Remember this is only one of twelve fish of silver.

23. First the craftsman uses a coarse rounded file, smoothing the edges and filing the tail. He always files the fish into a rounded form. As he says, "This is the way fish are actually formed." With a finer file, he continues to refine the tail. Small grooves are then cut in the tail with the *rayador,* the graver. The fish is held on the bench pin with a small hand clamp.

24. After he uses an even finer file to eliminate the file marks, he files the grooves again. In doing this he uses the round file first, then the three-sided file for the grooves and for further finishing.

FIGURE 10

25. He now uses a very fine emery paper to continue finishing.

26. With the graver, he makes lines on the fish (Figure 10). First he makes a line lengthwise across the body. Then he files this line and finishes the body further. The mouth is incised with a graver.

27. He puts a piece of paper on a small circular lead tablet and places the fish on top of it. The lead, the paper, and the fish are all clamped together with the hand clamp. The paper is used so that the lead will not discolor the silver. With a small, round-headed ball peen hammer, he stamps the eye of the fish, its pupil, and the scales (Figures 11 and 12). These are three separate stamps. They are $1\frac{1}{2}$ to 2 inches high and somewhat like thick, flat-ended nails. The stamp is in relief at the base of the cylinder.

Each day Sr. Cazares takes this stamping work home during his 11 o'clock breakfast (he has already been working for three hours). "It is more comfortable there and I do not waste time," he says.

28. With a knob-handled, sharp knife Sr. Cazares incises the fins more sharply. Then he delineates the grooves further with the graver. When he has filed the top of the tail about three times, the fish is done.

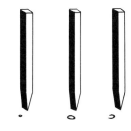

FIGURE 11

FIGURE 12

FISH OF SILVER

109

It has taken Sr. Cazares about one and a half hours so far and he has finished only one fish. There are three more to complete from today's mold. To finish the twelve-fish necklace, he still has eight other fish to make in two more castings. He also has not yet really done the silver chain work. It is a long, time-consuming process.

29. The silver wire for the chain (made at an earlier date usually) is spiralled around a circular stick. Each spiral is cut individually as needed. One spiral will be soldered to the nose of each fish to be attached later to the chain.

Taking a piece of flat charcoal, Sr. Cazares files a small area and places the fish on this spot. The charcoal reflects heat, making it easier to solder. He places a ring next to the nose of the fish. Near him is a container of borax with water, the flux. His solder is 2 parts silver to 1 part brass. Now with a kerosene lamp and a blower he solders the ring to the fish (Figures 13 and 14).

30. The ring-nosed fish is then usually put in a bath of sulfuric or muriatic acid called a pickle solution. This bath removes the fire scale (carbon) and oxidation. But because Sr. Cazares used the forge today and the fire is still hot, he uses the ancient method. He puts water, a little salt, and some lemon juice in a tempered clay cup. Put-

FIGURE 13

FIGURE **14**

FIGURE **15**

ting the fish in this solution, he sets it on the fire. "If the fire is already lit, this method is faster. It needs to heat only five minutes." He then removes the fish and rubs it with dry borax. Then he dips the fish two times in a little detergent with water to remove any grease. The pre-Conquest technique of cleaning silver involved using a substance from the maguey plant—a natural detergent which was used until several years ago.

31. Holding the fish in a handkerchief so his fingers will not touch the silver, he polishes the fish using a steel polisher, a steel rod which he first rubs over a smooth river stone. (Diamond dust can be used, but Sr. Cazares says the stone works just as well.) This is the final smoothing and finishing.

32. The chain for the necklace is made with coral stone and silver wire. The "coral" which is approximately $1/8$ by $3/8$ inches comes with a hole already drilled through it.

Since it is so difficult and time-consuming to stretch your own silver wire, I suggest you buy it. It has only to be the right size for your coral, but not too thick for the slender fish of silver.

Cut each wire length long enough to string 3 corals together and to make a hook at each end. There will be 23 groups of 3 corals. The fish will be connected by their ringed noses between every set of 3 corals, *after* the sixth set (Figure 15). The completed necklace is $19\frac{3}{4}$ inches long.

FISH OF SILVER

111

8 *THE COPPER OF SANTA CLARA*

Santa Clara del Cobre is located high in the mountains of Michoacán not far from Pátzcuaro (see Chapter 7). Officially named Villa Escalante for a regional hero of the Revolution, this unique town is still called by its traditional and more romantic name, Santa Clara of the Copper.

Although copperware is found in other parts of Mexico, none compares with the *martillado*, the hand-hammered, forged copper of Santa Clara (Plates 7 and 8). The thick *ollas* (pots) and trays of simple classic form are rarely made with any surface design. They need none, for the hammered, red-yellow copper makes a pattern of its own.

Santa Clara is a somber, austere town, especially so when it rains heavily as it did the day we visited. Like those of Pátzcuaro, many of its houses are immense. They hover about the plaza in a state of decay for they have been exposed to the rigors of this region for several hundred years.

The Santa Clarans inherited their craft from the pre-Conquest Tarascan Indians who knew the secrets of tempering copper and whose knowledge of metallurgy was among the most advanced in Mexico. Yet, this method of the *martillado* was brought by the Spanish. The great pre-Conquest copper mine of Hunguarán was re-opened when this work began, but its huge deposits were probably never adequately mined again. Today, while much copper is said to remain, the mine is no longer worked.

In archaic times, copper was used for the fine edges of tools. The molten red copper was formed in stone molds to make axes and chisels. Some copper tools were made with an alloy of tin; other copper was gold plated. Stonelets of copper as well as clay were used in rhythm instruments and tiny copper bells were made to be worn on the ankles and wrists, and on the costumes for the religious dances.

In pre-Conquest days the rich wore silver, the poor, copper. Because the conquerors and later the colonials both were mesmerized by gold and silver, copper remained the metal of the people.

The mining and working of copper ceased for a while after the Conquest. But in the sixteenth century when Don Vasco (see Chapter 6) arrived, he designated Santa Clara as the town of copper and brought artisans from Spain to re-teach the art and that of the *martillado* as well.

In colonial days and later, the *cobreros* and other craftsmen went to the city of Pátzcuaro each year for the great Fiesta of Salud (see Chapters 7 and 13). Here they performed a craft dance in which the artisans pantomined the movements of their work. There was a time in Santa Clara when copper played not only a great part in the economy of the town, but in the total life of the town as well. It still does, but not as much. This is an agricultural region, too.

During the revolutions in the nineteenth century, many mines were closed again and there were times when no copper could be had. It was then that the craftsmen began to buy used copper.

Today, the merging of copper with silver or gold and with wood is done in Taxco and Mexico City. Some copperwork is done in Cuernavaca, San Miguel de Allende, Puebla, and a few other towns, but it is completely different work from the Santa Clara *martillado*.

The working of the Santa Clara copper is demanding. The craftsman must build up his hands, wrists, and arms to withstand the force and strain of steady pounding on the metal (Figure 1). Besides having physical stamina, the craftsman must be familiar with the physical and chemical peculiarities of copper. He must be skilled in recognizing the condition of the metal as he beats, tempers, and shapes it, for copper becomes harder and more brittle as it is pounded until it can be shaped no more. The longer the craftsman works the metal, the more difficult his work becomes.

FIGURE 1

From the plaza of Santa Clara can be heard the insistent sounds of the beating of metal. Primitive forges are aflame in thirty to thirty-five patios and courtyards of the town. As many as eight to ten men are sometimes hired to work at a forge.

José María Ruiz and his family are said to be the best coppersmiths of the country. At their massive house a little girl was riding up and down on the ancient bellows. Several small children ran in and out around the smouldering forge, dodging the hot metal that was being lifted from the fire (Figure 2). The craftsmen work under a large covered area next to the patio.

Six of the Ruiz brothers work here. Although it is rare for a woman to engage in this craft because of the nature of the *martillado*, the one Ruiz sister was at work with her two brothers the day we visited them. The banging reverberated throughout the old house.

Though coppersmithing is traditional to Santa Clara, it was not to the Ruiz family. The family tradition began with José María and it may end with him. When José María inherited the large house from his parents, he had to devise a way to afford to keep it, so he began to work with copper.

"I taught myself by making the small pieces first," he said. "I made the small *cazos* [these are the traditional copper cooking pots with small handles on each side]. Twenty-eight years ago when I

FIGURE 2

began, there was no call for anything but these. Next I began making the small copper cups, then the larger ones for chocolate. I don't try to interest my children in copper. If they decide to go into it—alright. But meanwhile, they all go to school. They can choose to do what they want. Coppersmithing is a hard way to make a living."

José María took us inside the house to show us examples of his work. As we entered the huge living room, we tripped over rows of sprawling children. Among six brothers and one sister and their families, there are forty-two Ruiz children. Many of them were watching television with their grandmother.

José María showed us gigantic *vasijas*, vessels of all kinds: pitchers, *cazos*, and trays. In one corner stood an intricately-made, three-foot high church of copper. A huge tray displayed the Don Vasco de Quiroga coat-of-arms. Another tray, 1 meter long, contained a large dove. Some of the work was engraved or had a repoussé design, other pieces were fluted. All contained the pattern of the hammered copper, the *martillado*.

These last pieces had been made for the annual National Copper Fair of Santa Clara that is held each August. José María and his brother have won many prizes and their work is shown at the Museo de Artes Populares in Mexico City. They are recognized as the country's most skilled copper craftsmen.

Next José María took us into one of the three completely equipped kitchens in the house. Like the others, this one had a long table, a large refrigerator (by Mexican standards), and a restuarant-sized gas stove. Here they use their own ware for cooking. *Cazos* of all sizes hung on the wall. Chocolate cups, pitchers, and plates of copper were in the cupboards.

Copper remains a metal of the people. Sometimes one can still see a rancher with huge copper pots or tubs slung over his horse (or, more likely, in a ranch truck) returning to a remote ranch somewhere. Pitchers, jugs, shallow pans or trays, and washbasins (*compuestos de Jofaina*) are the traditional copperware of Mexico. Miniatures the size of thimbles or smaller are made for the children.

Cazos made in all sizes (Figure 3) can be seen on any market stand where food is served. At fiestas, *cazos* full of boiled chicken or soups send out tantalizing whiffs of ancient Mexican foods. The use of copper for cooking is an ancient as well as a modern practice for the

FIGURE 3

material disperses heat evenly. These pots used for cooking are coated inside with tin, a process called *estañarse*. Some of the *cazos* are many years old. They have been patched and repatched until the whole kettle has been rebuilt.

Copper is expensive. Although it is an item that lasts a lifetime, a large *cazo* can cost hundreds of pesos. The copper used in Santa Clara is therefore often secondhand, recovered scrap. It would cost José María 40 to 45 pesos a kilo to buy his copper new; for old copper, it is only 15 or 20, half the cost. Though copper is mined in Mexico today, it is used mainly for the manufacture of industrial and commercial products.

Because it is a conductor of electricity as well as heat, the copper that usually becomes the classic Santa Clara *martillado* is made from the discarded electrical coils, wires, and debris of the industrial age. Perhaps the fluted *olla* in the showroom came from the *bobinas* (coils) of generators from old cars, coils from refrigerators, or even the wires from electric lines. When Santa Clara first received electricity, the linemen could not keep ahead of the coppersmiths. As soon as the wire had been strung, the craftsmen removed it to use in their craft.

Across the street from the Ruiz brothers is the house of the Velasquez. Though they too are among the finest coppersmiths of Mexico, it is generally thought that the work of the Ruiz brothers is more refined. Perhaps it is merely the difference in styles, for the work of the Velasquez—also beautifully formed—appears more roughhewn.

We passed through the showroom-store, an enormous patio, then through the other side of the house to a second courtyard where the workshed and *fragua* (forge) were located. Here in the water-soaked workyard were several lean-to's where some of the workers live. About ten men were forging, tempering, and working the metal. Valesquez runs a larger operation than Ruiz.

After being taken from the medieval forge, four men bombarded the metal with sledgehammers, striking it with faultless split second timing, one right after the other. At one end a man with heavy tongs moved the red-hot copper between blows. Each person's performance was perfectly integrated with the action of the group. As in some fiendish diabolic rite, the fire behind them flashed and crackled in the forge. It seethed and fumed ejecting a fine black dust.

When we left, the sky was still leaden although the rain had slackened to a steadfast drizzle. Even as we drew away from Santa Clara, we could still hear the hammering of the copper in the distance.

FIGURE 4

The finished pieces we took with us were warm and graceful; they gave little indication of the physical stamina and prowess required by the relentless copper craft.

In the markets and plazas of other towns, *vendedores* can be seen selling a few pieces of the Santa Clara copper (see Figure 4). Every so often a man sits under the arcades with several rows of *cazos* and *vasijas* arranged geometrically before him in the ancient way. They are bought by the *campesinos* for practical use. At the same time in the museum-stores, markets, and fine stores throughout the country, others buy the same work solely for its beauty. The copper of Santa Clara del Cobre leads a double life.

There is no Working with the Craftsman section included in this chapter because of the difficulties and requirements of copperwork.

TIN AND BRASS 9

In San Miguel de Allende on the high central plateau of Mexico is the Llamas Hojalatería, the place where tin is worked. San Miguel is the center for this craft and the Llamas factory has been called the "Tiffany of Tin in Mexico." In the workshop you can hear the clatter and clang of the tinsmiths at work.

In its colonial heyday San Miguel had been a wealthy city, now prosperous townspeople, foreign residents, and visitors live in its ancient homes. It has become an art town and tin and brasswork have grown from a simple and modest pursuit into an art.

The Llamas tradition of tin making goes back only one generation to the father of the Llamas brothers who began a small tin shop in San Miguel in the 1920's. At first he made milk cans and other practical objects, but he changed his style at the urging of José Mojica, a great opera star and movie idol born in San Miguel. Mojica had returned to build a sumptuous Hollywood-style home and he urged the elder Llamas to do some ornamental tinwork for it. When Llamas demured, Mojica made a few models and asked him again. Still dubious, Llamas followed the Mojica models. They were successful and others wanted his work. Encouraged, Llamas experimented and began devising new decorative tin forms. This was the inception of the Llamas tin making for decorative use and the beginning of San Miguel's distinction in tinwork.

Today there are several small shops in San Miguel engaged in making ornamental tin and brasswork. But Llamas was the first; many of the San Miguel tinsmiths worked for and learned their craft from Llamas.

There were three Llamas sons: José, the eldest brother, who died; Eleuterio, who has the atelier and the shop which we visited; and Leonardo, who owns the shop next door. Leonardo has branched into wrought ironwork lately though he still does work in tin and brass. Every year Eleuterio works more and more with brass and less with tin although the two metals are often combined. Copper, too, is sometimes used.

The Llamas atelier is a large one by Mexican-handcrafts standards. Thirty or more men shape, hammer, and chisel the tin and brass while others are involved with shipping, packing, and distribution. Several women work in the shop closer to town.

The two-room store dazzles with floor-to-ceiling displays of gleaming *bibelots*, trays, mirrors, pitchers, lamps, jewelry boxes, and candelabra (Plate 9). Men are busy in the backroom packing tin and brass for shipment.

The Llamas Hojalateria is big business as well as a craft for the brothers sell wholesale in Mexico and the United States and they prepare special orders from all over the world.

Until last year the factory was housed in a colonial building at the south end of town. Today the tinsmiths work in a new factory that is light and airy. The personnel has doubled and the work has become more streamlined. Three men generally work together. At one table, they make brass and glass boxes; at another, tin and copper mirrors. Other workers form tin and brass lamps. In one corner a tinsmith molds brass hemispheres, while another solders their fine edges.

The workers, particularly those at the factory, are young. Perhaps when they have learned this exacting craft they will begin their own businesses as a young man named José has done. José makes the intricate, brass hanging lamps that a large atelier cannot often afford to make. He is about twenty-five years old now. After working several years for Llamas, he decided to start his own shop. He works in the cramped covered entrance, the two side front rooms, and the small patio of his house. His several children play in the same patio and his wife washes the clothes there.

Plate 1. *Ojo de Dios.*

Plate 2. *Nearika.*

PLATE 3. *Serape.*

PLATE 4. *Petates* are used here to wrap vendor's goods (foreground).

PLATE 5. The work of several craftsmen: A *Canasto* (left) and Corazón de Trigo (foreground). A black pot from Coyotepec and a *santo* rest on a *Petate* (right).

PLATE 6. Fishes of silver.

PLATE 7. Santa Clara copperware.

PLATE 8. Pitcher made of Santa Clara coppe

PLATE 9. The Llamas atelier displays tin and brass gift items.

PLATE 10. A Coyotepec marketplace displays the pottery of local craftsmen.

PLATE 11. The Tree of Life.

PLATE 12. Another and more intricate Tree of Life.

PLATE 13. Metepec Sun.

Plate 14. The *Virgen de la Salud*.

Plate 15. Batea.

PLATE 16. Papier-mâché mask.

PLATE 17. Papier-mâché figurine.

A neighbor told us about José. "I shouldn't even tell you about him. Now, we'll have to hear more banging. But I really don't care. He is an artist. He really makes these lamps the way they used to in San Miguel. It is a dying art. They are too difficult and it is too time-consuming to make them anymore. The tourists (Mexican as well as foreign) simply won't pay enough when they can buy the simpler lamps."

We ordered six brass lamps of the old style. The charge was about $50 for all of them. It was not enough for all the work involved. These lamps are made of opaque glass cut into hexagons—23 of them for a medium-sized lamp—which are edged with brass and then joined to form a globe. The even more complex stars are made of triangularly cut glass edged with brass and soldered together to form an 18-point star. At the Llamas factory very few of these lamps are made.

The Llamas tin tradition was largely an outgrowth of Spanish influence for tin was used sparingly in pre-Conquest Mexico and then not for ornamental purposes. It was cut or stamped in the form of a "T" and used as money, though barter was the predominant method of exchange in the great open markets of ancient Mexico.

The tin was obtained with difficulty from cassiterite in the mines of Taxco. It was reduced in simple terra cotta furnaces by charcoal fires and melted with copper to make bronze. Some tin was mined in Michoacán as well.

Brass was unknown though copper was common and widely used. Zinc, the metal combined with copper to make brass, was abundant, but it is possible that the pre-Conquest people did not know it was a metal.

In the days of the last emperors, metal craftsmen occupied a favored position in society, but their media were gold, silver, copper, and precious stones. They had developed a complicated, elegant art which has been revived only in the last thirty years or so.

It was the Spanish who introduced brass-making and who evidently taught the Indians how to use tin decoratively. Because gold and silver were the domain of the Conquistadores, brass, and particularly tin, were left mainly to the Indian and became mestizo crafts. Even today the art is dominated by colonial design. Tin and brasswork embellished as it is with curlicues spheres, helixes, scallops, and all kinds of tortuous convolutions has a baroque air.

In this high country of San Miguel lived the pre-Conquest Otomí

Indians. They were among the few not given to creative work since they were reportedly too busy fighting to develop their latent talents. The Spanish artistic influence was therefore most profound in this part of the country.

The Indian used tin and brass to suit his spiritual needs, a combination of his old religion and Catholicism. A commissioned miracle painter—there was at least one in every community—would paint the stories of personal miracles on tin (or copper, or canvas). These paintings called *retablos* were hung in church near the saint who had answered the supplicant's prayers. They were complicated and literal paintings sometimes bordering on the supernatural. *Retablos* are still painted and can be seen in the countryside churches. These primitive works are a vestige of a real folk art.

Still thriving, too, are the *milagros*. These "miracles" as they are called are small, thin, flat molds of silver and sometimes tin in the shape of legs, arms, hearts, and even eyes. Like the *retablos* they are hung near the appropriate saint.

Votive offerings looking like Christmas trees were often made of tin and garishly painted with a distinctive, transparent paint made by mixing the pigment with lacquer. Within the last year Llamas has developed a new style in painting his tin by using semi-gloss enamels to achieve rich, but muted colors.

Mexicans have been using tin cans for years to make many products. In Celaya, some of the most ingenious toys of the country are cut and devised from discarded cans (see Chapter 15). Recently on the Day of the Three Kings when many toys are sold in the markets for the children's Christmas, I saw small pails made from the tin shells of Eveready batteries. The advertising was the design. This is the *old* "pop art." Tin from cans is also used for tools: knives, spatulas, or gravers.

But the most celebrated tinwork is still that of San Miguel's Llamas atelier where the gleaming objects of tin and brass combine the metal of the people with genuine colonial artistry.

Working with the Craftsman

Javier Llamas, a nephew of Eleuterio Llamas, the owner of the atelier, offered to demonstrate the brass working techniques for us. To do so he made a lovely brass candelabra.

Tin, copper, and brass sheets are sent to the Llamas factory from Mexico City where they have been processed. Either brass or tin can be used for all parts of the candelabra although variations include combinations of either tin and brass, or brass and copper. Sometimes a tin candelabra is later painted.

Javier's candelabra is made of brass, tin was used only for the bottom of the cone. The brass has beauty in itself. If you wish to paint the candelabra, use tin instead. The candelabra can be made easily with either metal.

The design of the model is a classic one, but it may be simplified according to taste (Figure 1). The actual model was measured in centimeters which have been converted to inches (the nearest fourth). It is not necessary to follow the measurements exactly. They are intended only to give a general guide for the all-over shape and proportions. The completed candelabra is 11½ inches high and 13 inches across at its widest point.

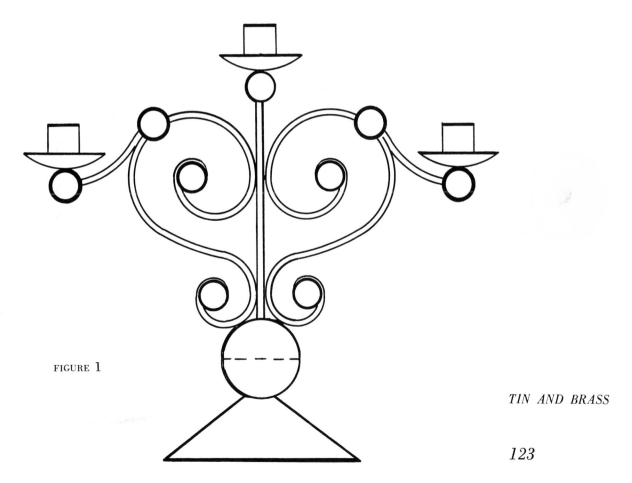

FIGURE 1

TIN AND BRASS

123

TOOLS AND MATERIALS

Brass and/or tin.

Galvanized wire, No. 12.

Tinsnips.

2 awls, one blunt tip, one pointed tip.

A compass for describing circles.

A ball peen hammer.

A metal puncher (hand punch).

Roundnosed pliers.

Various striated, hemispherical, and spiral *matrices.*

Replicas and patterns for particular parts of the candelabra.

Soldering tools and materials (an electric soldering iron can be used).

Muriatic acid (used in the soldering process).

A vise.

An anvil.

Sand.

Polishing tools and cloth.

Lacquer and brush applicator (plastic spray can be used).

A heavy rubber pad.

If you wish to paint a tin candelabra, you will need:
Anti-corrosive underpaint.

Semi-gloss enamels.

Brushes.

To antique, you will need:
Chapapote (a thin mixture of tar and gasoline, see Chapter 13).

Rags.

PROCEDURE

1. At the Llamas atelier the sheets of metal are cut with a foot-powered stamping machine. Tinsnips would do as well. Javier cuts a brass disc 6 inches in diameter for the cone at the base of the candelabra (Figure 2).

2. For a raised design on the cone, use the repoussé method in which the horizontal decoration is made by hammering on the reverse side of the metal over a depressed pattern.

Javier makes the grooves by measuring the design on a prototype of the cone and then delineating them on the brass with a compass (Figure 2). Next he places the brass right side up on a heavy rubber pad and depresses the ridges with a blunt-ended awl, using his shoulder to add pressure (Figure 3). Then he turns the brass upside down and, using the same instrument, he delineates a line half way between each of the two ridges (Figure 4). This raises the design.

FIGURE 2

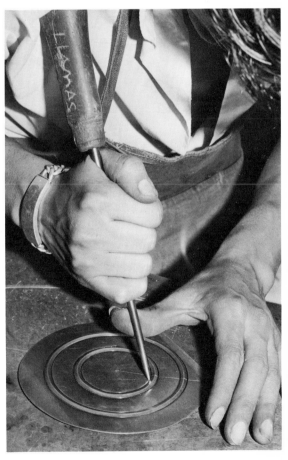

FIGURE 3

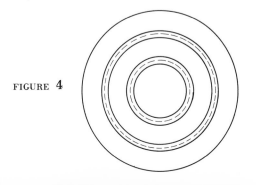

FIGURE 4

3. He puts the brass circle on an iron block and uses a hand punch, a *sacabocado*, to punch out the center (Figure 5).

4. Then he makes a "pie cut" into the brass, 3 inches across at the widest point of the cut (Figure 5). After this is done, he pounds the brass with a bar of roughly cut wood (1 foot long and 4 or 5 inches square), forcing the brass into a conical shape with the other hand as he pounds.

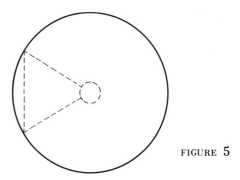

FIGURE 5

5. Tin is cut for the base of the cone, although brass can be used. Measure the bottom of the cone and allow a fraction of an inch more to be folded up over the side of the brass cone. Punch a small, thumbnail-size hole out of the metal (Figure 6) and save the punched-out disc. You will need it later.

FIGURE 6

6. Now on a large sheet of brass Javier marks and cuts 4 $\frac{1}{2}$-inch-wide strips, two are $17\frac{1}{4}$ inches long and two are $8\frac{1}{2}$ inches long. The two longer ones will become the larger curved rods. One of the shorter strips will be the central post, and the other (cut in half) will be the two smaller, lateral rods of the candelabra.

7. He sets the brass strips, two at a time, one on top of the other, on a striated iron block and pounds the brass into form with the blunt-ended awl.

8. Then he inserts a steel rod into each of the now partly formed brass tubes and with the bar of wood, pounds the brass into shape.

9. He cuts the galvanized wire to length. Size No. 12 wire is heavy and strong; he inserts this wire into the brass tubes to lend strength to the central post and the curved rods.

10. He places the tubes on the striated block again, pounds the brass more securely to the wire, and puts them aside.

11. Taking the brass sheet again, he measures the three candle-holders. Each strip is $3\frac{1}{2}$ inches long and 1 inch wide. Allow a fraction of an inch for a slight overlap. When soldered, these strips will form cylinders 1 inch in diameter. Allow a fraction of an inch more on the width of this metal to fold over the upper edge for a more finished look. The foldover must be pounded, but if you wish repoussé as in the model, this must be done now (see Step 2).

12. Now Javier puts the candleholders around a metal rod and pounds them into their cylindrical form (Figure 7).

FIGURE **7**

13. He solders each cylinder. All the soldering is done with an iron rod put into the orange and green flame of a gasoline lamp. When red hot, the iron is dipped onto the soldering material. The area to be soldered is cleaned with muriatic acid immediately before applying the solder. Javier used a glue-bottle brush to apply the acid. The soldering material is any low-melting, low-strength alloy used to bond higher-melting, dissimilar metals.

14. Then he solders each tubular rod down the length of the rod (Figure 8).

15. He pounds one end of each long rod to make its lowest curlicue (Figure 9).

16. He puts the larger section of the two-part spiral mold (that section forming the upper portion of the larger curved rod (Figure 10)) into a vise (Figure 11). He twists and forces the rod into its spiral form around the outside configuration, holding the rod to the mold with pliers and using his other hand to twist the rod into form. The smaller mold is used for the bottom spiral of the larger curved rod. Javier repeats the process for the second rod. The third rod will be left straight for it is the central post of the candelabra.

FIGURE 8

FIGURE 9

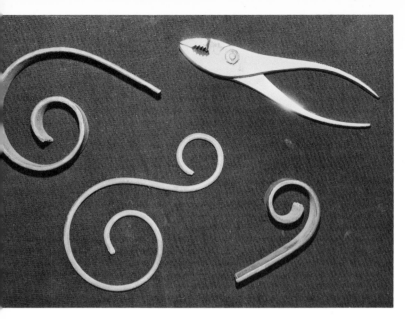

17. Now he hammers both curved rods on an iron block. He matches them to a replica, twisting them so they will have the right shape and angle. The final cinch is made with pliers. Then he turns the rod on each side and pounds it flat (see Figure 10).

I have seen the tinsmiths pound and shape these curlicues on an anvil without using a prototype. Without a mold it is slow, exacting work, but it can be done. You will need to draw a pattern for these curved rods no matter how you form them.

After being shaped, the larger rod is 5½ inches tall and 3 inches wide at its widest point, looking like half a "valentine." The rods are curved in opposite directions so that they form a complete "valentine" when attached to the central post.

The two larger curlicues must be shaped so that they will meet the central post of the candelabra about two-thirds of the way up the post and so that the bottom of the curlicue's lower curve will rest on the large foundation sphere.

18. Using a large metal pipe, about 4 inches in diameter, Javier pounds the smaller curved rods to shape, pulling one end straight (Figure 12). He matches these rods to a pattern. Javier follows several patterns that are etched on a tile.

FIGURE **12**

19. Next the brass is cut for the large sphere which rests on the cone. It must be molded into two halves or hemispheres. These will be joined later by soldering to form one sphere with a two-inch diameter. (Always cut your discs a little larger than the measurements given to allow for the spherical form and for the malleability of the metal. Some experimentation is advisable.)

The hemispheres are formed by hammering the tin or brass into a prototype. At the Llamas atelier the matrix was an iron cube with various sized holes looking very much like a giant iron die. The craftsman sat on a low stool and worked on a tree stump, the most secure table he could possibly use. He pounded the metal into shape by hammering a blunt-tipped awl against the brass that was set in the matrix. Other hemispherical matrices were formed in the stump itself (Figure 13). This method is ancient. Large numbers of identical beads were formed by pressing thin sheets of gold or silver over carved replicas or into carved matrices. In pre-Conquest Mexico these prototypes were made of wood, stone, horn, shell, bone, and metal. These methods of molding metals to shape and "raising" spheres and vessels from flat discs of sheet metal over a series of anvils are ancient methods still used by many Mexican craftsmen.

20. The hemispheres of the foundation sphere are soldered together.

21. Next the cone is soldered together. Javier files the top of the cone and looks to see that it is level. Now, turning the cone upside down, he solders the cone to the globe. (The globe is positioned so the seam runs horizontally.) At this point he also solders the tin base to the cone.

22. Then he pierces a hole at the top center of the globe for the central post to pass through. Inserting the post down to the bottom of the globe, he solders it securely to the top opening of the globe. (Remember to brush the area first with muriatic acid each time you solder. Then heat the iron and apply the solder.)

FIGURE 13

23. Now Javier puts the two large curved rods on each side of the central post, setting an iron block on the upper end to hold it steady. When he is sure the curlicues meet the central post where he wants them to, he solders each curved rod onto the central post (Figure 14).

24. After making sure the smaller rods are flat (see Step 17), he positions and solders them to the larger curved rods. They are soldered on the upper part of the outside curve of the larger rods. These small rods will support the two outside candleholders (see Figure 14).

25. Using another mold, he cuts three discs for the trays of the candleholders. They are 2½ inches in diameter. You will need another prototype in which to shape these gently curving trays. They are slightly flanged.

Marking direct center through a perforation in the prototype, Javier uses it as a guide for the central placement of the candleholder. He solders each of the three holders to the trays, both inside and outside.

Javier borrows a torch attached to a gas tank to melt this solder since the depressions are difficult to reach with the iron. He cools each area afterwards by pouring water from a tequila bottle into the tray and holder.

26. He now pours sand into the base cone. The punched-out piece of tin that was saved earlier is then soldered back into place. The sand

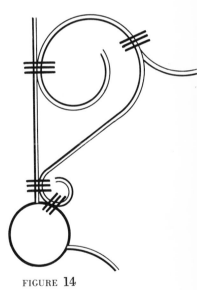

FIGURE 14

TIN AND BRASS

131

gives the candelabra stability. Pour in as much as possible so that the sand won't shift when the candelabra is moved.

27. The soldered trays and candleholders are polished while their surfaces are still easy to reach before being soldered to the candelabra.

28. After they are polished, Javier makes a hole at the bottom of each tray for the insertion of the candelabra rods. He solders the trays in place, leveling them by eye before the material sets (Figure 15).

29. Now is the time to make the eighteen hemispheres of brass for the nine spheres that will be soldered to the tops of the curlicues and to the central post. (In addition to being decorative, these balls are useful in covering some of the soldered areas and the ends of the rods. They also provide a base for the candleholders.)

These hemispheres will all be 1 inch in diameter, but again, allow for the spherical form and the malleability of the metal. Experiment first. You will need a matrix on which to shape them.

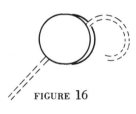

FIGURE 16

30. Javier then solders on the eighteen hemispheres—nine on the front of the candelabra and nine on the back. Each pair forms a globe. Each globe will have a space in between its two halves to allow for the passage of the rod (Figure 16).

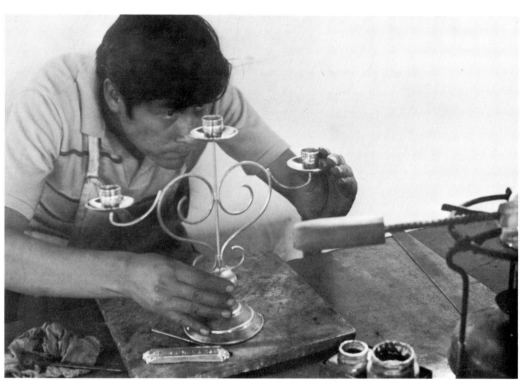

FIGURE 15

FIGURE 17

Using a strip of tin to brace the hemispheres (Figure 17), he begins to solder each hemisphere to the rod; first one side of the candelabra, then the other. Beginning with the lower four central hemispheres, he solders the upper three central hemispheres next. Last, he solders the outer two.

It has taken Javier two hours to make the candelabra. It is basically finished.

31. The candelabra is washed with soap and water and dipped into a box of sawdust to dry. It is rubbed until no moisture remains.

32. The time-consuming polishing process is next. At the Llamas atelier some of the polishing is done by electric belt with interchangeable pads. For the candelabra, a soft lamb's wool pad was used. (Used carefully, the home electric shoe polisher should work well.)

33. Next the candelabra is polished by hand with a soft cloth.

34. At the atelier lacquer is then applied with a brush to insure continued brilliancy. (Plastic spray will work as well.)

35. As mentioned earlier, Llamas has developed a new way of painting his tinwork. First he paints the tin with a creamy gray anti-corrosive paint. Then he uses commercial semi-gloss enamel in muted colors. Next he applies *chapapote* (a thin mixture of tar and gasoline) with a cloth. This is wiped off with another cloth before the mixture dries, leaving the tin with a slightly antiqued look. When dry, it is lacquered.

The traditional painting of the tin is a transparent gaudy and garish color achieved by the use of powdered pigments (called *anilinas*) mixed with lacquer. Remember, if you paint your candelabra, use tin.

PART

IV

CLAY

THE BLACK POTTERY
OF COYOTEPEC 10

Before the Palacio Municipal in the large, quiet plaza of San Bartolo de Coyotepec stood two large shipments of black *cántaros* (round water jugs) waiting to be delivered by bus to Oaxaca. Coyotepec is a center for the famous black pottery of Mexico (Plate 10).

Few people were on the streets when we asked directions to the house of Doña Rosa, the town's most celebrated potter, whose work is known all over Mexico.

We found Doña Rosa to be a woman in her seventies. She is small and lean weighing no more than eighty-five or ninety pounds. Her *rebozo* was wrapped turban-style, the long ends falling down in back. A filmy scarf protected her embroidered *huipil* and her long skirt. She worked with astonishing power for her small size, but then she has been a potter all her life.

There are those who say Rosa Real de Nieto is only a performer today. Seated on a *petate* she works in the large tiled arcade of her new home. Before her, in a semi-circle, are fifteen or twenty blue chairs for the groups of tourists who come to buy and to watch her work. She no longer sells to the local population as the other Coyotepec potters do, but only to the tourists and entrepreneurs who come to her. Her work is found all over Mexico and is in collections throughout the world.

Until last year, Doña Rosa had lived on the same dirt road in a simple, dirt-floor cottage. Two decades ago, she could be seen sitting in the doorways of Oaxaca with her husband on market day. They sold *cántaros* and *tinajas de mescal*, the traditional pots of Coyotepec that they had brought in from the country. She was one of many potters who followed a tradition almost unchanged from pre-Conquest days. Although she still follows these traditions, she also makes animal figures such as perforated owls, many bells, and all kinds of trays, bowls, vases, and other objects.

Doña Rosa claims that success came to her one day in 1952 when she accidentally scratched a dried, but unfired, pot with a stone. She fired it anyway and when the scratched area turned deep black, she took another pot, rubbed a larger portion with stone, and fired that one. It, too, became deep black. The pottery of Coyotepec had always been various shades of gray, but now it was gleaming jet. Thus it is to be believed that the lustrous blackware of Coyotepec and Doña Rosa's fame arose simultaneously.

The burnishing of pottery, however, is not new. It was done in Mexico centuries ago before the time of Monte Albán, that great Zapotec Indian civilization whose impressive ruins still preside above the city of Oaxaca. Although the application of designs with quartz (or obsidian) on blackware appears to have been rare, a typical piece of Zapotec pottery, a burnished, gray spherical jug, was similar to the *cántaro* which is the model for this chapter (Figure 1).

Doña Rosa evidently rediscovered the ancient techniques of polishing the gray clay. As the modern innovator she has received national recognition and won many prizes, not only for the burnishing of clay, but for her beautifully formed ware. When he was President

FIGURE 1

of Mexico, López Mateos visited her and many photographs of his visit hang on her patio walls.

Doña Rosa did not, however, discover the method for making black pottery. Perhaps it was confusion over terms that led to this misconception, for blackware or black pottery refers to the traditional dark gray or gunmetal clay that is fired here.

"It has always been done," she will tell you. Whether burnished or not, the blackware has been produced in the Oaxaca region for at least 3000 years. Centuries ago the Indians of Oaxaca obtained gray clay by controlling their fires; it is done the same way today. Although blackware was apparently once formed by open firing, it has been fired in pit kilns for many years.

Any clay can be fired black if it contains iron oxide. The ware becomes black if the fire is smothered with mud or soil and if the fire exhausts the oxygen in the kiln when the oxides are reduced. To the extent that the ware is reduced (deoxidized) it will be gray or dark gray, or black. It is only the burnishing that provides the lustrous black by forcing the molecular bodies of the clay into parallel position before it is completely dry.

Because Coyotepec clay is very fine-grained, it is fragile and must be preheated, fired, and cooled much more slowly than most clays. It cannot be fired at high temperatures. To allow for reduction, the fire must be sealed while much of the unburned fuel remains and a fairly constant firing atmosphere must be maintained and closely watched. When reduction is not a consideration, the firing is a much simpler and shorter process.

To make her fires, Doña Rosa uses *encima,* the hardy oak used for making oxcarts and wheels, and another wood called *jarilla.* Although she claims these woods must be used, others say that these particular woods are not necessary.

"The wood must be dry to smoke," she explained. "A low fire is made first, then it is made hotter and hotter for ten hours. But if the fire becomes too hot, the pottery will not be black."

A piece of blackware can be fired buff, black, and then buff again (Figure 2). These colors can be alternated indefinitely by varying the firing methods. Much of the lower part of one side of the *cántaro* model (see Figure 1) is buff because this portion became too hot.

"But it is one way to tell if you have authentic blackware," explained Doña Rosa.

FIGURE 2

It has been said that some potters here use a "slip" of black shoe polish or graphite from batteries to make their pots black. If this is so, it saves them a lot of trouble in building the complicated fire. Some potters in other parts of Mexico achieve the same general result by using a slip containing a very fine manganese dioxide. This slip can be burnished before firing, producing an even glossier surface than that of the natural Coyotepec clay.

Doña Rosa's kiln is a large pit about 10 feet deep. Other kilns in Coyotepec are similar, only smaller. To reach the opening of the sunken kiln, a roomsized well has been dug with earthen steps leading to it. The fire is in the bottom two-thirds of the kiln. The greenware, or raw clayware, is placed on the strong adobe platform into which 3 wedge-shaped holes are incised. Two logs reinforce the platform. Large pieces of broken pottery are placed on the clay to be fired. Above this, the kiln is sealed with clay.

"How do you know when the fire is right?" I asked Doña Rosa. "I look at it. I tell by looking."

She fires at night, a customary practice, for when it is dark it is possible to test the fire with a pitch stick to see if there is a smoky, yellow flame. To the scientist this would indicate reduction. Doña Rosa just knows what to look for because years of experience have taught her. Like most of Mexico's potters, she does not work with small degrees of difference in temperatures or other properties. Centuries of trial and error, and accumulated knowledge, have taught the potter what to do and how to use his materials. Little firing is done during the summer rains. The wood is wet and the pit kiln is surrounded by soggy earth which causes the clay to crack and break.

Raw clay is brought in from the country a few kilometers away on the backs of burros or by oxcart. The dark gray clumps of dirt are wrapped in packs made of large *petates* (see Chapter 4) stitched with split reed or rope. Though the raw clay is tinged dark gray, this is merely coincidence; the gray color is organically produced and it burns out in the firing.

Doña Rosa keeps her clay loosely covered with asbestos in a brick pit a few feet from her patio. It is taken from here, put on a large *petate*, and treaded with bare feet for ten hours. (Others in Coyotepec say the clay is worked only two or three hours). Doña Rosa's nephews and grandchildren do this job. Her son often joins them, for besides being her business manager, he too is a potter.

Her tools are simple: a flat, blackware bowl filled with water, a few broken pieces of pottery, a couple of discs, a piece of tin, a strip of leather, and some clay.

A tour bus arrived and another group wandered in and began to sit before Doña Rosa. As she started to make yet another *cántaro*, we left to visit another *taller*.

Passing the potters' cooperative, we walked back to the plaza and entered a small store that sold black pottery of all descriptions. The owner, a jolly woman, took us through the store into the back compound. Her husband was not there for he had gone off early in the morning to bring in more clay. Although the women model the clay, it is the men's work to collect, prepare, and fire it. The Matamoros tree of life potters and the Metepec potters (Chapters 11 and 12) are all men. A few women, however, make dishes.

In a large room off the dirt courtyard stood many baskets of *monos*, the small toys Mexico loves so well. Next to these was a pile of figurines: small birds, pigs, cows, dogs, and other fanciful animals all containing whistles in their tails. Another basket held dozens of ingeniously shaped bells.

Ceramics was a highly skilled art in pre-Conquest Mexico and figurines about 2 to 3 inches in height were a common sight: fish, ducks, monkeys, jaguars, birds, men, and, it is thought, little gods of rain, corn, fire, fertility, and so on. Some were wonderfully mechanical such as the clay birds which dipped their beaks into water when perched on a bowl and monkeys that whistled when given a drink. Some of these were mass-produced by molds or stamps. Whether they were talismen, idols, or just toys is not known. It has been suggested that each family may have had a collection of these little figures, or that they were made for a large pilgrim trade, souvenirs of a once-in-a-lifetime trip to one of the great holy cities. For whatever reason they were made, there were hundreds of thousands of them and they are still being found. They are still being made in many parts of Mexico, too—wherever there is clay. Some new figures are buried awhile and passed off as antiques.

We bought fifty or sixty contemporary *monos* for twenty centavos apiece to use as Christmas tree decorations. As we helped the lady wipe kiln soot from the figures, we thought we smelled shoe polish on the cloth, but we could not be sure.

In addition to the *monos*, there were the traditional four-sided bells shaped like Maltese crosses, and black jugs perforated with three-cornered or ovoid holes. And on the table were the traditional *tinajas de mescal*: the round jugs webbed with brightly colored maguey fiber (or more recently, string). Near the top of the web, a small cup is secured, and on the other side is a cord which can be strung to the *campesino*'s belt or to his burro. These little "portable bars" hold *mescal,* a potent and popular drink. Distilled from the maguey, some of the best *mescal* comes from the Oaxaca region.

Stacked in a corner were several *cántaros*, the historical clay water jug. This gracefully shaped spherical *olla* with the narrow lip has been carried on the shoulders of the women of Mexico for centuries. Not long ago, in central Mexico, I saw twenty or thirty women carrying red clay *cántaros* up the hill from the town water fountain. These *cántaros* are large; they hold several liters of water.

The classic, beautifully shaped *cántaro* provides one of the oldest services on earth and is the product of one of the world's and Mexico's oldest crafts.

Working with the Craftsman

TOOLS AND MATERIALS

Clay. The clay used for the *cántaro* must contain iron oxide if it is to be fired black. It must also contain very fine-grained colloids if the pottery is to be burnished.

A porous slab.

A piece of broken pottery.

A strip of leather.

A piece of tin.

Two rounded discs of the same size.

A bowl of water.

A kiln. An electric kiln cannot be used because it will automatically oxidize the clay. A gas kiln or even a primitive kiln is more suitable. For a primitive kiln, make a low brick wall on the ground, setting the bricks in a circle. Put in the ware set closely together and cover well with broken pieces of pottery. Then seal with clay—or as some potters still do in Mexico, seal with manure. This will keep the oxygen from entering the kiln, a necessary condition for reduction.

For more technical information, refer to any good comprehensive book on ceramics (see pages 243-45).

All the measurements given for the finished *cántaro* (as well as for the Matamoros tree of life and the Metepec sun in Chapters 11 and 12) are measurements after firing. A 10 percent shrinkage is usually figured in the firing of Mexican clays. However, the shrinkage of the reader's clay may differ.

PROCEDURE

1. Dipping her hands in water, Doña Rosa kneads a large chunk of clay about 12 by 7 inches for 2 minutes or so (Figure 3).
2. She breaks off a quarter of this clay and sets it aside.
3. The remainder is shaped into a cylindrical ball.
4. Holding this ball in one hand, she begins to punch out the center with her other fist, an action resembling a baseball player punching

THE BLACK POTTERY OF COYOTEPEC

FIGURE 3

FIGURE 4

his mitt (Figure 4). This takes great strength. (An ancient method still used in parts of Mexico achieves the same result using concentric rings. Beginning with a small, circular pat of clay pinched up around the perimeter, successive strips of clay are placed inside this rim and smoothed upward to raise the sides.)

5. At the moment, Doña Rosa's hand is her wheel. As the cavity is formed, she turns the clay on her fist while she slaps the outside clay with her other hand (Figure 4). When finished with this process, she sets the beginning *cántaro* aside, face down.

6. With a primitive potter's wheel, she works the crude *cántaro* into shape. The wheel is nothing more than two round-bottomed, clay discs; the first is placed face down, the second sits upright on the bottom disc. The top disc then turns on the first one (Figure 5).

7. Now she places the *cántaro* on this simple wheel.

8. Slowly turning the *cántaro* on the wheel, she works the clay until it is even in thickness and form (see Figure 6). The walls are a little over $\frac{1}{4}$ inch thick. The main body of the *cántaro* is $7\frac{1}{2}$ inches high (excluding the neck); it is 4 inches across the base and 9 inches at its greatest width (or 28 inches around).

9. From the clay set aside, she takes chunks and evens the thickness of the walls from the *inside* of the *cántaro*, (Figure 6).

FIGURE 5

FIGURE 6

10. Then taking a broken piece of pottery, she smooths the inside. (All the tools except the tin are kept in water when they are not being used.)

11. By applying pressure from the inside, she makes the clay form spherical. This is the basic shape of the *cántaro*; it is the final modeling of its basic shape.

By now much of the excess surface water on the clay has evaporated and the consistency has changed. Doña Rosa works under a covered patio so the wind will not affect the clay, drying it too quickly and causing cracks. This is particularly necessary in hot, dry areas such as that of Oaxaca in the winter. For the same reason, she places her clay on a porous surface when not working with it.

12. Lifting the *cántaro* and the top wheel disc together (the *cántaro* remains on this disc) Doña Rosa sets them aside. Then from the extra

THE BLACK POTTERY OF COYOTEPEC

145

clay, she takes another piece slightly larger than her fist and kneads it for a minute or so.

13. She rolls it between her fingers until it is about 1½ inches in diameter and 13 inches long. This clay rope is then set on the remaining extra clay. It is wet enough so that it has a squishy sound when she works it.

14. Now placing the top disc (with the *cántaro* still on it) back on the inverted disc, she pinches in the top of the *cántaro* and scores it with her fingers. (The *cántaro* is on the wheel from this point through Step 22.)

15. She places the roll of clay on the scored rim, pulling and working it up as she turns the wheel. This will be a cylinder 3 inches high. (Allow some extra for overlapping.) Its thickness is uniform except where the clay is joined (Figure 7).

16. Wetting her hands again, she smooths this area and widens it.

17. From the water bowl, she takes a strip of leather.

18. Twirling the pot, she uses the wet leather to smooth the clay and to give the top of the *cántaro* its final form. She raises and widens the opening so that it is 3 inches across the neck.

19. With the leather, she makes the thick lip of the *cántaro* (Figure 8). She pushes down with the index finger, other fingers following, and pushes up with her thumb. The lip is flared 1 inch; it is ½ inch

FIGURE 7

FIGURE 8

thick. The height of the finished *cántaro* is 8½ inches. It has taken Doña Rosa about 20 minutes to make this *cántaro*, but she has been making them for 60 years. Like all the other potters I have watched, Doña Rosa makes absolutely no wasted movements.

20. The *cántaro* is set aside in the shade away from the wind for four days until it has a leathery consistency. In rainy weather it will take longer.

21. After four days, Doña Rosa scrapes the "dried" clay with a dry strip of tin until it is smooth (Figure 9). The tin strip is cut from a tin can.

22. Four days later (a total of eight days), she hand rubs the *cántaro* with a piece of quartz (Figure 10). This is the process that gives the clay its lustrous sheen.

Often, only an area design is burnished rather than the whole pot. This is usually a design of two diamonds separated by a floral pattern (see Figure 11).

All Doña Rosa's work is signed which is rare in a country where the craftsman is usually anonymous. On the bottom of the *cántaro* model is printed "Doña Rosa, S.B. Coyotepec, Oax.-Mexico." But be-

THE BLACK
POTTERY OF
COYOTEPEC

147

FIGURE 9

FIGURE 10

FIGURE 11

cause she never went to school, her son incises the signature with quartz, cutting into the clay rather than scraping as Doña Rosa did for the design.

23. After another fifteen days, the *cántaro* is fired using the complicated technique described earlier. The burnished *cántaro* must be as dry as possible before firing, otherwise the luster can be destroyed by shrinkage during firing.

Whether or not you wish to try making a *smoky* pot, you will have made one of Mexico's oldest artifacts—the ancient *cántaro*.

11 *TREE OF LIFE*

Not far from Izucar de Matamoros in the State of Puebla is the Santa María Tonantzintla Church, a church known for its pasteboard motifs. Doll-like angels and archangels, apostles, saints, and virgins that look like toys are set against backgrounds of clouds, shells, vines, fruit, flowers, and suns. The scenes are really a type of Mexican baroque. Some say the potters of the trees of life of Izucar de Matamoros were influenced by this church. In Metepec, which is also renowned for its trees of life, it is said a local church was influential in their design, too.

Although the Metepec tree of life is better known, it is generally conceded that Metepec copied the work of Matamoros, though they did so in their own way and developed their own archetypes. The trees of Matamoros are more "authentic" and they have a longer history, although this medium-sized town in the center of an agricultural region is not a large pottery center.

The tree of life is a simple (Plate 11) or intricate (Plate 12) clay form which projects a single motif in great decorative detail. Its form is more or less that of a tree and it usually holds candles. In Matamoros the tree of life is traditionally used in ceremonies for churches, weddings, and funerals to hold candles or sometimes incense.

The decorative possibilities for the tree of life are endless:

150

branches, tendrils, fruits, vines; anything and everything is put on it, in it, or hung from it—even when the theme is death. Somehow the tree of death is just as happy as its counterpart. These trees are made with ghoulish white skeletons with carmine lips and piercing amber eyes attended by crowned skulls and other cavernous figures. With their ever-present flowers, they are not at all morbid. The Mexicans have always accepted the fact that death is part of life. The tradition of the tree of death comes from Matamoros, but contrary to popular belief, Matamoros makes the tree of life most of the time.

The Matamoros tree of life has been called one of the most notable productions of Mexican art. Originally made in Huaquechula, Puebla, and in parts of the State of Morelos, it has been made in Matamoros and nearby villages such as Amozoc since the emigration of the potters to those areas.

One of the earliest symbols of fertility and rebirth, the tree of life supposedly came from the Middle East by way of the Moors to Spain. From Spain the concept, with its Judeo-Christian adaptations came to the Americas. The tree of life is, of course, associated with the Old Testament story.

The clay tree of life did not appear until after the Conquest. Its original motifs were religious. Leaf-clad Adams and Eves are still used most often. Other trees have moon crescents with angel faces, hot pink apples suspended on wires, and serpents lurking in jungle-like trees. It may be filled with fantastically hued birds and butterflies or crowned lions leering from the branches. On top, a superb angel may hold the world. Still others depict the Flight to Egypt or the story of the Nativity. Medallions, swags, garlands, and even columns straight out of the European renaissance and the baroque era are used.

Pre-Conquest design was geometric and symmetrical, but with the Spanish came not only entirely different concepts of life, but a completely different art style as well. The comingling of Spanish and Indian traditions which followed produced a unique Mexican style.

In the nineteenth century, many trees of life were made with patriotic motifs. *Viva La Independencia* and *Viva Mexico* were emblazoned on banners across the breadth of the wide trees. Flags, coats-of-arms, and political figures of the day were depicted along with the usual spray of flowers, vines, and birds. Gilt and oil paints were used then and the colors were more muted than they are today.

The trees were also more solid looking then with thicker branches. Today's trees from Metepec have round, chunky figures that are almost voluptuous. Those from Matamoros are as individual as they were long ago. Their branches have a tubular appearance though they are solid. The figures are not so exuberant as those of Metepec for the shapes are more controlled and more refined.

The Metepec colors of several years ago were harsher than those of today which are lighter, brighter, and gayer probably because of the advent of new commercial pigments. They are still gaudy, however, and each part of the tree—one flower or one bird—is a solid color, sometimes embellished with gold. The exception is the art of Mónico Soteño who has broken away from the customary Metepec style by painting his trees with linear design on a white background. The effect is light and delicate.

A few years ago I saw two gigantic trees, one painted in a combination of blue, green, aqua, and purple; the other in pink, orange, melon, and red. They had been ordered from Metepec by Neiman Marcus for their Christmas decorations and had cost thousands of dollars. In the Museo de Artes Populares, commissioned trees are ten feet tall. Although such trees can cost between $400 and $1000, most trees cost less than a dollar.

The story persists that at one time the artist, Diego Rivera, helped Metepec with her use of colors. No one knew much about this, but one representative in Metepec said, "Perhaps it was the other way around. Maybe he got some of his inspiration from us. We have always used wild colors. Look at the Otomí women. Their skirt is one color, their belt another, and their blouse still another color. It has been this way since earliest times."

Brilliant as they are, the colors of Matamoros are not so completely abandoned as those of Metepec. They claim to use earth colors and secret ingredients. Their trees are decorated in linear designs over a variety of base colors. The old Matamoros trees—and there are quite a few around—have a muted color now. They have probably faded, for in a color photograph of a Matamoros tree printed thirty years ago, the colors are as bright as those used today although they were earth tones of cream, ochre, sienna, and green.

Trees to commemorate a special occasion can be ordered in either Matamoros or Metepec as long as there are enough "subjects" relative to the event to make decorating a tree possible. Since the Mexican Olympics of 1968, a few people involved with the games have ordered "Olympic" trees. The possible subjects are legion: the Olympic torchbearer, high divers, gymnasts, pole vaulters, swimmers, bicyclists, etc.

A particularly entrancing and fairly new tree is one with a sea motif: octupi, fish, little clams, oysters with pearls, mermaids, seahorses, turtles, and snails lay in a background of seaweed, leaves, and flowers.

In Acatlán, a town a few miles south of Matamoros, Herón Martinez fashions very sophisticated trees. Once this town made only ordinary clay ware: banks in the image of bulls and burros, and a few *candeleros* (candlesticks). Today complicated structures are built using a multitude of motifs: clay acrobats balance each other at dizzying heights, and animals are poised one on top of the other, each succeeding one smaller than the next. Some of these intricate forms go back to pre-Conquest designs.

Some of these trees, which are actually sculptures, reach a spread of six feet through the center. Many are hand polished to a rich patina of red-brown. The clay of Acatlán is extremely durable, almost metallic—it rings like a bell when flicked with the fingernail. These are all Herón Martinez' creations and he has become very successful with them.

But Aurelio Flores of Izucar de Matamoros constructs the most traditional tree of life in the country. He lives in a tropical compound on a dirt path away from the one or two paved streets of the town. Sr. Flores works in a dark adobe, one-room *taller* with a simple reed roof and a dirt floor. Two more rooms built around the bare dirt compound are the family's living quarters. The buildings have no windows and there is little furniture. The Flores family sleep on *petates* and cook on a charcoal stove.

Aurelio Flores is seventy-three years old although he looks much younger (see Figure 1). He has made these trees and a few other figures for sixty years as did his father before him. His early years were difficult, however.

"Work stopped during the Revolution of 1910—the Revolution of Madero. Hardly before we started in 1912, the Carranza-Zapata Revolution began and typhus came. Work stopped. When this was over and we began to work again, then 1918 came and with it the flu epidemic. Many houses in town were closed. Whole families died. It was a long while before we could begin once more. Many of our customs died then, too."

Just down the road lives Heriberto Castillo, the only other person in town who still makes the trees of life. Renowned throughout Mexico for their work, neither Sr. Flores nor Sr. Castillo were known to the passersby from whom we asked directions.

The Castillo family appears to be fairly wealthy for they live in the mestizo manner and have extensive living and working quarters. Their output is more varied and more refined than that of Sr. Flores who works in the old tradition. His work is the same as it was when he began years ago.

Heriberto Castillo's family stopped working during the hard times, too. When life became normal again, an entrepreneur from Puebla asked the family to make the trees for him. Since the family of Sr. Castillo's mother had been potters and she remembered how the trees were made, they began again. (Sr. Castillo's father was a foreigner, he said. He was born a few miles away.)

The same businessman asked Aurelio Flores to work for him and for twenty-eight years he made his trees of life and sent them to the city of Puebla. Through this proprietor he won second prize in a craft exhibition in the United States. The grateful store owner gave him a heavy serape, some bolts of cloth, and a large bag of hard candy. Though Sr. Flores betrayed no disdain for this treatment, the incident is typical. Mexico's craftsmen still find themselves at the mercy of middlemen.

Both craftsmen sell now through the Museo de Artes Populares but like the other men who sell to the Museo (or the Banco Fomento), they sell also to their own clientele.

Recently the Museo sent a photograph to Sr. Flores of a set of figures his father had made before the Revolution, asking if he could make them again. Using his memory and the photograph as a guide, Sr. Flores was making the set when we were there. The figures stood about six inches high and were placed in two rows on a board. Freshly painted, they were still wet. When we returned the following week, these little figures were varnished and they stood waiting to be taken to Mexico City.

Sr. Flores makes the trees of death only on special order and in October to prepare for the Day of the Dead celebrated on November 2. Although similar to our Halloween, the holiday in Mexico is still a religious one. The idea, however, is the same: spirits and ghosts. On this day the women carry the *funerales*, the trees of death, as well as food to the cemetery to share with their departed family members. Sr. Flores says he does not make his trees with moribund figures unless they are specially ordered. His *funerales* are made just like the trees of life except that they are painted black.

In this region, the mourners at every funeral used to carry a black tree of death in the cortege to be left with candles lit at the gravesite. This tradition stopped in 1918, however.

A happier tradition was the use of the tree of life at weddings; the theme was Adam and Eve in the Garden of Eden. Each family, the bride's and the groom's, ordered two trees. Two were always included in the wedding photograph and they were also used in the ceremony itself. This tradition, too, disappeared after 1918. Sr. Flores looked for a picture of this, but old photographs are hard to find. Most have been lost through dampness or eaten by rodents.

An unusual custom does still exist here, however. Each year for the day of San Pedro and San Paulo, Sr. Flores makes twelve trees of life. They are ritual trees made like the others except that censers are placed on the trees instead of candleholders. The twelve trees represent the twelve apostles and twelve men are chosen by the *mayordomo* (chairman of the town fiestas) to carry these trees in the religious procession to the church. But it becomes more complicated. Two special churches are in Matamoros, that of San Pedro and that of San Paulo, one on each side of the town. Matamoros is divided into fourteen *barrios*, seven on each side of town. Each year the twelve men are chosen from one side to carry the trees to the church on the other side of town. The following year, the whole procedure is reversed.

The *mayordomo* is the protector of the trees; they are kept in his house. With the addition of twelve trees each year, he undoubtedly has a fine collection, for according to Sr. Flores, the *mayordomo* of Matamoros is not changed each year.

Working with the Craftsman

TOOLS AND MATERIALS

Clay. Since the trunk and branches of the Matamoros tree are solid, you will need to use a sandy clay. Sr. Flores brings his clay in by burro "from above, on the plain." It takes four hours for him and his son to bring it in. To prepare it, they stamp the clay with their feet for six hours.

A porous slab.

A clay hammer.

A mold, a bowl with a handle inside.

Galvanized wire, #14. Instead of galvanized wire, you may use Kanthal wire, which will fire at 2000° F. But remember, a low fire must be used for the sandy clay and the galvanized wire should fire up to about 1500° F.

Regular wire for cutting the clay.

Pliers.

A small metal spatula. Sr. Flores made his from a tin can.

A bowl of water.

A container of sand.

A straight stick, used to measure the height of the tree.

A round stick, a smooth, round stick about ½ inch in circumference.

Molds, a flower, a leaf.

PROPORTIONS

The tree of life is 8½ inches high by 7½ inches wide. The candle-holder is one-third the tree's height and the branches are two-thirds its height. The widest point, between the spread of the branches, is the same as the height of the tree *minus* the base. The base is one-quarter of the height of the tree.

PROCEDURE

1. Seated on a *petate* on the dirt of his *taller*, Sr. Flores kneads a mass of clay about 8 inches in diameter. He then takes a quarter of this clay and kneads it further.

2. He forms the kneaded clay into a ball and pats it into a thick pancake with his hands (Figure 1).

3. He sets the pancake on the porous slab and, after dipping his homemade clay hammer in sand, he pounds and flattens the clay which will be the hemispheric base of the tree of life. It is ¼ inch thick, 2 inches high, and 4½ inches in diameter (or 12 inches in circumference). Allow for its spherical shape.

4. Dipping the pancake in sand, he places it sand side down on the mold which is basically the same size as the base. Sr. Flores made his own mold (see Figure 2). It has a handle inside. (A half gourd

FIGURE 1

FIGURE 2

of the correct size can be used.) The mold in Figure 5 in Chapter 12 is similar to Sr. Flores'. Holding the mold by the handle between his feet, Sr. Flores forms the clay over it (Figure 3). (In the next chapter, "Metepec Sun," the craftsman holds this kind of mold between his knees.)

5. Dipping his fingers in water again, he smooths the clay.

6. With the clay still on the mold over his toes, Sr. Flores slices off the extra clay around the edge of the mold by means of a wire which he holds between his teeth. He then sets the base aside; it is still on the mold.

7. After kneading more clay from the original mass, he makes a roll 3¾ inches long and 3 inches in circumference (Figure 4) which will be the trunk of the tree of life. It is solid as are the branches. (Metepec, in contrast, forms its trunks and branches in a mold. They are hollow.)

FIGURE 3

FIGURE 4

Note: Anytime you are working with clay always knead the new working piece, water it with dampened fingers, and pinch the clay area to which it will be attached. Then add the new piece and smooth it with wet fingers. All non-metal tools are always kept in a bowl of water so they will be wet when they are needed.

8. Sr. Flores roughens a large area at the top of the base and raises a small mound which will later hold the bird. It is raised just in front of the section where the trunk will be set. On each side of the base, $\frac{1}{4}$ inch from the bottom, he pinches up the area to receive the branches (see Figure 5).

9. The trunk is placed on the center of the base (Figure 5). (Do not be concerned if it is not centered exactly; Sr. Flores' trunk was not; it is part of the charm of the handcrafted object.)

10. He adds small pieces of extra clay, working them in around the base of the trunk. He then smooths the joined area and the base with his tin spatula which has been dipped in water first. (While working on the small tree of life, Sr. Flores is also building a large tree. He makes two trees in a morning. Beginning at 6 A.M., he is finished by noon. Working on both at the same time, he is not idle while waiting the few minutes necessary for the clay to dry between processes. Sr. Flores never makes an unnecessary move.)

FIGURE 5

11. He takes more clay and kneads it briefly, making another roll about 15 inches long and 2½ inches in circumference. This will make a branch. After it is rolled, it is slightly flattened so that its measurements are 15 by 1 by ½ inches. It, too, is solid.

12. He cuts the roll in half with his wire. (When Sr. Flores is not using this wire, he holds it between his toes.) Each of these 7½-inch-long rolls will be a branch of the tree. The branch, however, is 5¾ inches high when measured from the base of the tree after it is formed and placed in position.

13. He affixes one end of the left branch to the base of the tree and then attaches the upper end of the branch a little below the top of the trunk (see Figure 6).

As noted earlier, the placement of the branches of the Matamoros tree is unique—a kind of inverted valentine form. This is one way the reader can recognize a Matamoros tree. Another way to tell the Matamoros tree is to see if the branches are "flattened," rather than circular such as those from Metepec. The trunk of this Matamoros tree, however, is round.

14. The right branch is positioned in the same way as the left (Step 13).

15. The *mechero*, the actual candleholder, is formed from a roll

FIGURE 6

of clay 2 inches long and 4 inches in circumference. Always make the clay a little longer to allow for overlapping.

16. Sr. Flores pokes a round stick about ½ inch in circumference through the center of the roll of clay.

17. With the stick through the center, he rolls the clay. As he does so, the hole becomes larger. He stops when the opening reaches 1 inch. When completed, the *mechero* will look something like a giant noodle (Figure 7).

While the candleholder dries for a few minutes, Sr. Flores returns to work on the larger tree. Then he smoothes the branches of the model.

18. Now the *mechero* is placed on the top of the tree trunk (remember to follow the rules in Step 7). After positioning the *mechero*, he uses a straight stick to check the height of his tree (Figure 8).

19. Sr. Flores takes another piece of clay, a small piece, and begins to form the bird.

It is difficult to explain how the bird is formed. The clay is bent at right angles in the center. Then, with a few deft movements of the fingers, he adds only a pinch of clay for the beak and the basic form is completed (Figure 9). The wing is made later. He sets the bird aside, for though it is made early, the bird is one of the last additions to the tree. The bird is 3 inches from beak to tail. The circumference of its body at its greatest part is 3 inches.

FIGURE 7

FIGURE 8

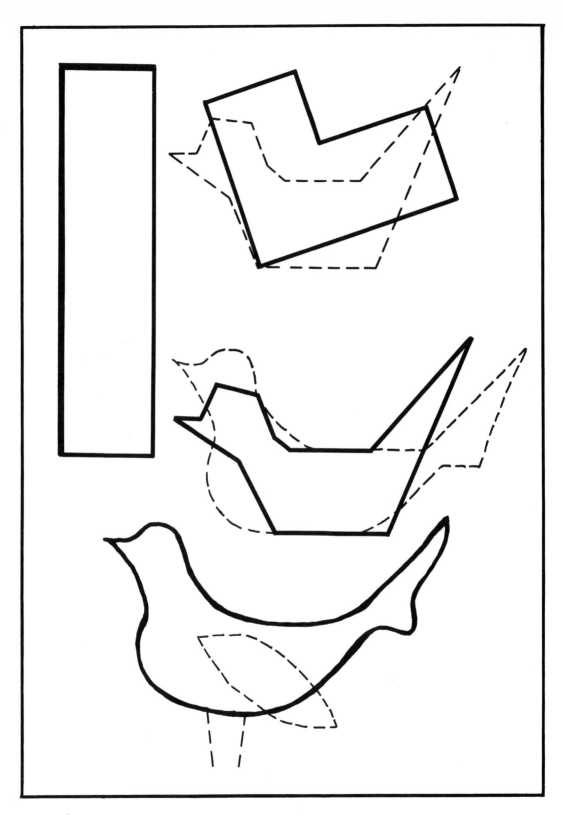

FIGURE 9

20. He takes another handful of clay and kneads it, taking only a small part to make a flower.

21. Sr. Flores chooses a flower mold from among many (Figure 10). Although some molds are handed down from generation to generation, these molds have been made by the potter.

22. First he dips the mold in sand, then he slaps it into the clay (Figure 11). The mold is a mere impression of the flower which, with its stems and leaves, is 2 inches high and 2 inches at its greatest width.

23. Holding the wire in his teeth, Sr. Flores cuts out the flower around the mold, but merely cuts a circle around the form (Figure 12).

FIGURE 10

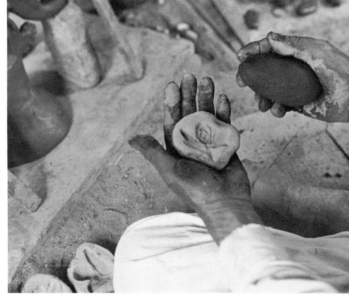

FIGURE 11

FIGURE 12

24. Next he slices off the extra clay from the bottom of the flower. It is cut almost wafer thin.

25. He smooths the clay and shapes the flower with his fingers. This is the major part of the modeling of the flower. The mold is only a guide.

Some of Mexico's potters scorn the use of molds. Teodora Blanco of Atzompa is one of them. She fingerforms her flowers completely. Beginning with a roll of clay, she bends the tip and then taking successive portions from the bottom of the roll, she deftly forms each petal separately.

26. Sr. Flores uses another mold for the two leaves. It is two inches high and 1 inch at its greatest width. (Follow Steps 22 through 25.) He sets the leaves aside.

27. With two tiny balls of clay, he makes two oval drops, 1½ by 2 inches in circumference, which will be the fruit of the tree.

28. The flower is now affixed to the trunk just below the *mechero*. Prepare and score the area first, press the flower on, add more clay, and smooth (see Figure 14).

29. With regular pliers he cuts four wires, each about 1 inch long, from a roll of #14 galvanized wire (or Kanthal wire). The wire is used to attach the ornaments to the tree.

30. First he places two wires for each leaf in the branches about 1¾ inches from the *mechero* (Figure 13). He then sets the leaves into the wires (see Figure 14).

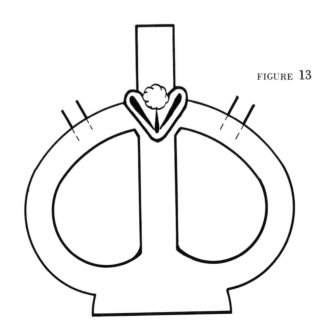

FIGURE 13

FIGURE 14

FIGURE 15

31. Now he cuts two more lengths of wire about 2 inches long. These will hold the fruit 1½ inches from the trunk. He inserts one end into the underside of each branch leaving the other end free (see Figure 14).

32. He cuts two more lengths of wire, 1½ inches each, for the feet of the bird. Put the two wires into the base of the tree on the mound that was raised in Step 8.

33. The bird is now placed on the wires (Figure 14). He should stand free of the trunk.

34. Two more wires are cut, 1½ inches each. One is inserted into each fruit, making a loop (be sure the clay is dry enough to do this.) Then connect the fruit to the hooks on the underside of the branches.

35. The wing which Sr. Flores made before is now put on the bird (see Figure 14). It is 1 by ½ inches.

36. After the tree has been dried in the shade for fifteen days, it is ready for firing. Sr. Flores builds a bark fire. "It is expensive— 19 pesos a *costal* [sack]. But it produces a strong fire." The tree is fired for six hours and then left in the kiln for a day. Sr. Flores' kiln is a primitive one (Figure 15).

TREE OF LIFE

165

Do not be upset if the tree cracks during firing. Sr. Flores has this problem too, especially with his larger trees. To help avoid this problem, he uses wire in the main pole and major branches of the larger trees. If the tree cracks, he uses a mastic to repair the break. It is stronger than the clay itself, and when painted over, no one can tell the difference.

37. With zinc oxide, *blanco de española* (whiting) and his secret ingredients, Sr. Flores undercoats the entire tree. (Though he fires twice, the reader could really fire only once by using a white coating after the first firing and then painting the tree as it is done in Metepec.)

38. After the undercoat is applied, the tree is fired for two hours in a low fire. It is left to cool for another three hours. Aurelio Flores is the only potter we visited who fired his ware twice, unless Sr. Castillo of Matamoros does too.)

39. Now the tree is ready to be painted. It may be left plain or it may be painted white with *gesso*. (It can also be sprayed white.) The true Matamoros tree, however, abounds in color and overcolor of linear design. When painting, be sure the wet paints do not mix. Use a different brush for each color.

40. Sr. Flores uses his own brushes: burro tail attached to a simple stick by thread. "I make my own colors, so I have to make the brushes also, to go with them. My colors are the colors of the earth, mixed with my secrets," he said pointing to his head. His secrets must be fantastic for he achieves brilliant colors of all kinds which are usually associated only with synthetics. Sr. Castillo buys vegetable pigments in the Merced Market in Mexico City.

For the color and design of the tree of life, see Plates 11 and 12. Your design does not have to be exactly the same, but study these examples to get a general idea and then devise your own scheme.

41. Sr. Flores makes his own varnish. This is also a secret recipe. A characteristic of the Matamoros tree is its cream color base, created by the yellowish varnish over the undercoat. I would suggest that the reader spray his tree with lacquer or plastic—rapidly—so the colors will not run.

Sr. Flores usually spends two weeks forming his trees and two weeks firing, repairing, painting, and varnishing them, a month altogether for the finished product.

I would suggest, again, that you paint your tree with many colors and overcolors so you will have a tree of life in Mexico's most traditional style, that of Izucar de Matamoros.

METEPEC SUN 12

The small compound of Timoteo González Degollado in Metepec overflows with clay saints and churches, angels and lions, doves and suns. Clay roosters cover the courtyard wall, a row of benign padres meditates on the low roof, and mythical animals are suspended beneath the balconies. Hanging from hooks on every wall are the Metepec suns (Figure 1).

Timoteo González works in a small, dark room sitting on a narrow board on the dirt floor with his feet in a small pit.

"Little by little I do these," he said as he modelled a two-foot high St. Francis. With the tip of a large bolt, he impressed the folds of the cassock (Figure 2).

Printed on the second-story wall of Sr. González' house are the words "The House of the Great Timoteo." The letters are fading, but this does not seem to bother him. Sr. González, a septagenarian, has worked since he was five years old. Born in the *barrio* of San Mateo, he was a member of an old family which began making the allegorical figures of clay at the end of the nineteenth century.

"My parents and my grandparents were potters. They made the *cazuelas*, the small figures, the *sirenas* [mythological sirens], and the figures for the *Natividad*."

167

FIGURE 1

Metepec is 51 kilometers from Mexico City and only 7 kilometers from the famous market city of Toluca. It is and has always been an important pottery center. Many of its citizens still make the earthenware jars and bowls for the everyday use of the local and surrounding population. On the roofs of several houses we could see the red *cazuelas*, the *ollas*, the *cántaros*, and the *jarritos* drying.

For many years Metepec made polychromed figures of the Three Kings, Joseph and Mary, the infant Jesus, and other religious symbols

CRAFTS OF MEXICO

168

FIGURE 2

especially for the *Nacimiento*, the crêche that every family sets up for Christmas. Then the craftsmen began making secular figures. Among them were the flamboyant peacock, the symbol of the immortal soul, and the double-headed eagle, said to have come from the Hapsburg coat-of-arms.

When the Metepec potters found new forms they liked and that were successful, they made a mold. Some of these molds have been passed down from father to son and are greatly prized, but new molds are still being made constantly.

The original "toys" of Metepec, it is said, were conceived to fill a spiritual need of the people. Their own religion had been taken away by the Spanish and the people needed something with which to make new religious offerings. Whatever it was, the object had to be cheap enough so that the people could afford it. The clay figures of Metepec filled this need.

Perhaps these religious objects are an outgrowth of the pre-Conquest idols (see Chapter 10), but no relationship has been established, particularly since no one knows for what the ancient figures really were used. Whatever their function, the making of toys is not new to Metepec. In the Museo Antropológico Nacional is a clay toy on wheels dated A.D. 650.

Although the religious clay polychromes of Metepec are traditional, many objects made here today are new. New or old, Metepec art is satirical, bizarre, and baroque. A mixture of paganism and Christianity, Spanish and Indian, it is a free, enthusiastic, vigorous, and individualistic interpretation of legends, customs, symbols, flora, and fauna. The result is extravagant fantasy. The Metepec work has been called the most truly baroque expression of art in Mexico today. Metepec whimsy is found all over the country and the world. Sophisticated Mexico City residents and then tourists discovered Metepec several years ago. Since then the potters have been busy devising new designs to keep up with the demand with the result that fewer traditional forms can be found each year. Because they are constantly creating new designs, lapses in good taste occur occasionally in such items as Porky Pig banks and Disney-like rabbits. Even Sr. González had rows of bloated, striated pig figures drying on his patio. The King of the Forest, the gay skeletons garlanded with bright flowers, biblical scenes, Noah's arks, the suns surrounded by chunky leaves and flowers, warrior angels on horses—and trees of life, abound.

In fact, one of Metepec's claims to fame is its tree of life (see Chapter 11). It is said that the sculptured tree of life on the facade of the church at Ixtapan de la Sal was Metepec's inspiration. A government representative for the *artesanías* of the State of Mexico explained, "The church's tree was to show 'the original sin.' But the Indian couldn't understand this. This was life, so when he copied it he added the birds and the flowers—all the happy things. This is your Mexican tree of life!"

Although the *Nacimiento* is still the customary yuletide decoration, some Mexico City people began to buy the trees in place of the *Nacimiento*. Metepec does a thriving Christmas business supplying the city and others at this season. For the Day of the Dead, they sell many frivolous figures of death.

The Metepec toys can be either exuberant in their motifs or quite simple, but their colors are always spectacularly unrestrained. This is one of the reasons Metepec ware is so enchanting. The Mexican has never been afraid of color. He lives in a country of wild, natural hues from the jungles of the *tierra caliente* to the rain-soaked mountain peaks—he seems particularly unafraid of color in Metepec.

Many of the town's craftsmen maintain successful *talleres*. In his narrow compound surrounded by storerooms, lean-to's, and workshops, Heriberto Ortega makes fanciful polychromes, one of which won second prize a few years ago in an international exhibition in Milan. Mónico Soteño (see Chapter 11) who paints his ware in a different style from the others is becoming successful. The Escarcega house, near the town square, makes a finely decorated plate of dark greens and yellow on a terra cotta base of which whole sets can be ordered. The Fernandez factory, where many trees of life are made, is a large one although all the work is done by hand.

Sr. González claims he was the first to make the Metepec suns which radiate in profusion on his patio walls. Measuring 7 inches to 2 feet across, they are rimmed by leaf-like rays. Their expressions range from the austere and scowling, to the droll and mirthful (Plate 13).

Although the spiritual concept of the sun played an important part in pre-Conquest life, it has little to do with Metepec's polychromatic clay suns of today. Today's humble Metepec sun is made mainly for *cantinas*, the simple, usually unadorned bar of the *campesino*. Sophisticated citizens put the suns in their patios. Asked why the *cantinas* buy them, Sr. González said he didn't know, "but a sun makes people happy."

Working with the Craftsman

TOOLS AND MATERIALS

Clay.

A mold.

Dry sand.

A maceta, the clay hammer.

A knife.

A container of water.

A stick, much like the cuticle stick.

A cortador, a large homemade cheese cutter.

PROCEDURE

Although Sr. González usually works in his *taller*, he moved outside so that we could take photographs more easily. For this reason, he made the clay sun directly on his cement patio.

Because Metepec clay is porous and therefore not strong, Sr. González mixes together four or five clays, all of which come from several kilometers away. The powder of the feathery *plumilla* (the dried red flower of the tule from the Río Lerma) is added to make the clay more cohesive. The clay is then pummelled with the *piedra de moler*, a large, round smooth stone, and sifted. After this it is mixed with water and prepared.

1. Sr. González first puts sand on the work area and then, dipping his fingers in water, he kneads a cubed chunk of clay about 8 by 11 inches.

2. After separating half of the kneaded clay, he kneads it again for half a minute or so and makes a ball of clay which he sets aside.

3. He dips the clay hammer, the *maceta*, into the sand and then uses it to flatten the clay until it is about 10 inches in diameter and ¼ inch thick (Figure 3). This action is called *tortillear*—to flatten like a tortilla.

4. He then models the clay over the mold which is a rounded clay "bowl" with a handle on the inside center (Figures 4 and 5). He puts the mold on his knees, holding it by its handle. The mold is 7 inches in diameter and about 1½ inches deep. These will also be the dimensions of the sun.

FIGURE 3

FIGURE 4

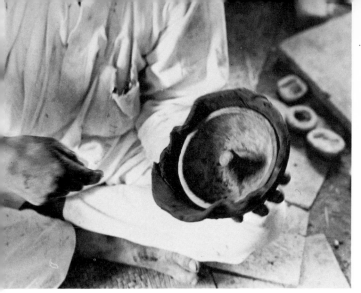

FIGURE 5

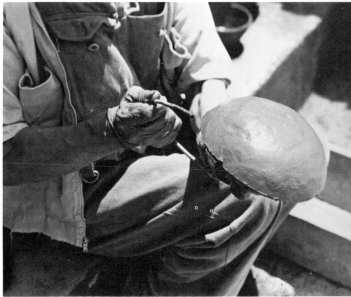

FIGURE 6

5. He dips his fingers in water and smooths the clay.

6. With a large homemade cheese cutter, the *cortador*, he cuts off the extra clay around the edge of the mold (Figure 6).

7. Still holding the mold on his knees, he takes part of this excess clay and makes a roll about ½ inch thick. You will need about 15 inches of rolled clay altogether. (Remember to dip your fingers in water each time you work with a new piece of clay.)

8. Break off two lengths of clay, 3 inches each, and place them firmly on the sun 2 inches in from the perimeter to make the eyebrows (see Figure 7). Dip your fingers in water and add a little extra clay around the edges and press.

FIGURE 7

FIGURE 8

FIGURE 9

9. Now break another length from the roll, about $2\frac{1}{4}$ inches, and apply the nose (see Figure 7). Dip your fingers in water again and work in the edges as in Step 8.

10. Separate four small pieces of the roll for the eyelids. The two top lids will be $1\frac{3}{4}$ inches long, and the bottom lids, $1\frac{1}{2}$ inches long. The measurements of both are $\frac{1}{2}$ inch high and wide (Figures 7 and 8).

11. Roll two small balls, $\frac{1}{2}$ inch in diameter, for the eyeballs. Place them between the lids (Figure 8).

12. With a stick that has been dipped in water first, make striations on the eyebrows. Sr. González' stick looked like a large cuticle stick (Figures 8 and 9).

13. Make deep pupils in the eyes with the same stick (see Figure 9).

14. Flare the bottom of the nose by pinching out each side about ½ inch and then make deep nostrils with the same stick.

15. With a roll, 4 inches long and ½ inch thick, make the top lip—it is smiling (remember to apply using the method described in Step 8).

16. With another roll, add the bottom lip. It is the same size as the upper lip, but it is set differently (see Figure 9).

17. Roll 10 balls, each about 1 inch in diameter (see Figure 9). These will form about half of the rays you will need for the perimeter of the sun.

18. Each ray is placed separately around the sun. Sr. González begins just left of center and places the rays clockwise, still holding the sun on the mold between his knees (Figure 9). If he is called away, he hands the mold to one of his children who holds the clay in the shade.

Each ball is set 1½ inches in from the edge. While placing it, Sr. González bends each ray slightly forward, twisting it at a little different angle from the last. Then he twists each one a little more and smooths it with water. Each ray stands up and away from the surface of the sun (see Figure 10).

19. While another son holds the form which is still on the mold, Sr. González rolls 6 more balls for the rest of the rays and sets them in the same manner (Figure 10).

FIGURE 10

20. To remove the mold, Sr. González holds the sun while his son gently takes the mold out from under it. (You will need a helper to do this.) The sun is then set on a board.

Because this piece has been made in the sun, it has probably been drying faster than it would otherwise have dried. The reader may have to wait a few minutes longer before removing the mold.

21. With the sun now on a board, Sr. González striates each ray with his fingernail, always dipping his fingers in water first (see Figure 11).

22. Now with a small knife (such as a jackknife), he cuts out the area between the lips and smooths it with a wet stick (Figure 11) and then with his fingers.

23. Next he cuts out the area between the eyebrows and the eyes (Figure 12), and repeats the process described in Step 22.

FIGURE 11

FIGURE 12

24. With the stick, he makes a hole at the top of the sun into which string will be inserted later. On each side of the hole, he inserts a wire, putting an extra piece of clay over each insertion point. The wire which forms a 1-inch loop will later serve for hanging the figure.

25. He dries the sun in the shade for two days and then fires it for three hours. This is the only firing that is done. (Some of the Metepec figures are reportedly "fired" only in the sun.)

26. To build the fire, Sr. González ignites wood and old shoe soles (cut into small pieces) which he buys from the *zapatero*, the shoemaker. "It builds a stronger fire," he said. He places the pottery close together in the kiln. After firing, the pottery is left in the kiln for a day to cool.

27. When the sun has cooled, a mixture of *cola* (mucilage from fish tails or more often animal debris from slaughterhouses), *blanco de españa* (whiting or calcium carbonate), and water is painted on. This mixture is the homemade Mexican version of *gesso*. The reader can easily substitute commercial *gesso*.

28. Colors are applied with commercial one-inch brushes (Figure 13). Sr. González uses common aniline pigments which he mixes with industrial alcohol to make strong and permanent colors that do not fade.

FIGURE 13

The color is put on haphazardly at first, leaving spaces between the color strokes to prevent bleeding. Use a different brush for each color. Fill in the remaining areas more carefully after the colors are dry.

Although its use in Metepec is relatively new, gold paint is sometimes applied over the other colors with a fine brush for additional decoration. It is not mixed with industrial alcohol because it comes already prepared.

The more varied and vibrant your colors are, the more your sun will be characteristic of the Metepec figures. But the sun can also be left its natural clay color, or it can be left white. Whichever you choose, no lacquer is used on the Metepec clay.

Sr. González painted the color directly on the clay; the model did not have a base coat. One of the colors was a specially prepared metallic green and although the effect was pleasing, the colors would have been more brilliant if a base coat had been used.

Because of the time involved in waiting for the Metepec sun to dry, the finished painted model in Plate 13 necessarily had to be different from the one Sr. González made before the camera. I chose one as similar as possible to the original, but as in all handwork, each piece is somewhat different. (This situation is also true of the black *cántaro* of Coyotepec, Chapter 10, and the Matamoros tree of life, Chapter 11.)

PART V

WOOD

SANTO 13

Each region in Mexico has its *santero*, a woodworker who carves the local saints for the villages and the church. The *santero* is the wood sculptor of the people. He will make a *santo* (saint), a cross, an ornate door, perhaps a mask, or whatever else is ordered.

Apaseo el Alto, Guanajuato, a small town in the Bajio backed by jagged cliffs, is a center for wood-carvers and the home of Domingo Galván, one of Mexico's master *santeros*. His work is found throughout the country. Sr. Galván's *taller* is evidence of his industriousness —*santos* are everywhere. Some are molds, others have already been carved. In the patio, a St. Francis is being carved and glued together piece by piece. Along the corridor, ancient saints hang from the walls. Large patterns drawn on brown paper hang from a wire as do old prints of saints from magazines, books, and calendars. Two narrow door panels carved with flowers and saints lean against the wall.

Most of the pieces are well designed, but the best are the careful copies of colonial Spanish-inspired saints. The flowers and other adornments are the same as they were when first introduced, for the *santeros* still work in the colonial tradition. The carving of the *santo* is a Spanish and now a mestizo art. Because Apaseo el Alto is in the heartland of the area once occupied by the Spanish, it is part of the region in which their influence was most strongly felt. The first craftsmen were imported from Spain.

Woodcarving was one of the fine arts in pre-Conquest Mexico where the carvers were held in high regard. It is said they worked under special conditions, separated from their families, because the idols they made were sacred—the gods lived in them. The *santero* today does not work under any special conditions, but his *santos* too, are greatly revered. In this respect, there is little difference.

Ancient Mexico was covered with thick forests of exotic and extremely durable woods. The high country had great stands of oak, sycamore, walnut, cedar, and cypress, while the lowlands provided mahogany. Finely carved wood decorated the pyramids and the temples, but this work has not survived the years as the stonework has. Much of Mexico's timber, however, was destroyed by the Spanish and has never been completely restored. "The Indians bring the wood down to us from the mountains," said Sr. Galván. "It used to grow near here. Now it is farther away."

The churches that were built to the new god and the saints brought by the Spanish had to be adorned. The Indian wood-carver became an expert. With the new tools of iron and steel that were better and easier to work with than the old, he made florid carvings of cherubs, angels, saints, vines, flowers, volutes, filigrees, columns, and garlands—all the rich carvings for the altars, the church facades, and the ecclesiastical furniture. He made the decoration more important than the architecture and he readily adopted the Moorish and the Spanish-European forms, mingling them with his own tradition as usual. The result was an entirely new style.

In one corner of Sr. Galván's *taller* stood two *santos*, San Felipe and San Luis Rey. The first had a fiber cord around his waist and a crown of thorns on his head. The other in painted aqua breeches and gray leggings wore a gray and gold crown. These two carvings were made in the best tradition of the *santo*.

"They are for the church," said Sr. Galván. "When a saint is ordered for the church here, it will not be antiqued. It is the others I sell to who want their saints to look old—I sell to different stores in Mexico and to the United States. It is these customers who demand the antiquing. If the church has a new saint, they want him to look new!"

When he began in 1935, Domingo Galván was the first in Apaseo to carve *santos*. Disillusioned by previous endeavors, he had gone to nearby Querétaro which had been one of the colonial centers for the production of religious art in Mexico. He worked and studied in the religious workshop that was still there at the time.

Originally, his family made hand-rolled cigarettes, but big business undercut their prices forcing them out of work. They then turned to making shoes and then to carpentry. Each time, larger factories lured their customers away. It was Domingo Galván who began to make the *santos* for by now he had learned how to work with wood. The twenty *santeros* who have their shops in Apaseo today were once his apprentices. They all learned their trade from him.

"I usually have about six men working for me. I pay them by the piece," he said. "The others are apprentices—two or three of them are good. It takes five or six months to learn the craft. But the most important thing is one must like the work or one can never become a fine *santero*." Sr. Galván had about fifteen men working for him when we were there.

The story of Mexico's *santos* is mainly that of the myriad virgins who appeared miraculously after the Spanish arrived.

The Virgin of Guadalupe, Mexico's Virgin Mary and patron saint, was the first. She is possibly the most ubiquitous religious figure in the land. Though there are some disbelievers, every bus, taxi, and most cars in Mexico carry her image. She is in virtually every home, workshop, and store; she is certainly in every church.

She was the dark-skinned virgin who is said to have appeared one day before a poor, simple Indian. The stones beneath her feet gleamed like precious jewels and celestial music accompanied her appearance. After a few more miracles occurred raising frenzied interest among the people, Juan de Zumárraga, the first Archbishop to Mexico, officially recognized the apparition.

The Virgin had materialized on the site of the Shrine of Tonantzín, the venerated Indian mother of earth and corn, a shrine Zumárraga previously had destroyed. Today it is the place of the great Shrine of Guadalupe. The Archbishop who had burned the priceless Aztec manuscripts had in one swoop, bridged the chasm between Spanish Christianity and Indian paganism. The two have existed together successfully ever since.

Other miracles began to appear around the land. Loved and revered to this day, these saints have great followings.

The Virgin of Ocotlán appeared next, promising water to a severely drought-stricken area. Tlaxcala's Virgin of the Burning Pine

Tree appeared inside a pine tree. The Virgin of Solitude, *Soledad,* was discovered in a burro train.

Some *santas* were brought from Spain. The Virgin of Remedios was carried under the doublet of a soldier in Cortés' army. She was small, about one foot high, and crudely made of wood. Each year great pilgrimages are made to Cholula where she resides.

The Virgin of Zapopan was taken to Jalisco in the sixteenth century by a Franciscan friar (see Chapter 1). She still takes yearly journeys around Guadalajara and wherever she goes, fiestas are held and dancers and musicians follow. Her wardrobe is one of the finest cloth and the most precious jewels. As so many of Mexico's *santas,* the Virgin of Zapopan requires a full time valet to care for her silks, satins, and brocades.

Some of the original saints are made of fine porcelain, a product and an art brought from Spain. Others are crudely fashioned from wood or from a *pasta de Michoacán,* a cornstalk paste mixed with the glue of the orchid used from ancient times by the Tarascan Indians to make their idols.

The appearance of the Virgen de la Salud (the model made in this chapter, see Plate 14) is a romantic story. A life-size figure of a beautiful woman made from *pasta de Michoacán,* she was found floating in a canoe on Lake Pátzcuaro. Today, she watches serenely over her broad domain from the Basilica in the highest part of the city of Pátzcuaro, where a fiesta is held in her honor every year. Many pilgrims come and there are parades, fireworks, novenas, and masses.

The Virgen de la Salud is attributed to have the power of healing (see Chapter 7), but miraculous powers are seen in all the virgins. Thousands of people travel each year to San Juan de los Lagos for special favor from the virgin there.

The Virgin of San Juan de los Lagos has a moon at her feet as does the Virgin of Health and so many others. The inclusion of the moon may have arisen from a Moorish tradition or perhaps was a concession to pre-Conquest worship. Or it is from the Assumption of the Virgin Mary as she rose to heaven, the moon at her feet, a crown of stars at her head. No one seems to be sure of its significance.

There must be hundreds of *santas* in Mexico for every town has its favorite benefactress as do many families. Add to these the many saints who must have come readymade to Mexico and one can see that the *santero* is assured of customers.

The use of *santos* was widespread in colonial days but many of the haciendas, chapels, and shrines of that period have been left to decay since revolutionary days. In some of these buildings, *santos* have been left to weather, to split, to disintegrate. Hundreds stand where they were abandoned years ago. If one knows the area and the people, one can still collect them. These hardy *santos* made of the wood of the country are the same saints made in Apaseo el Alto today.

Working with the Craftsman

TOOLS AND MATERIALS

2 saws, one regular-sized saw, one cut-off saw.

2 chisels, a small one and a large one (1½ inches wide). The chisels are twisted files, honed at the ends to make a cutting edge. Files are often used to make knives in Mexico as the steel of the file is extremely strong.

A large knife.

A machete.

A coarse file in a wooden (*colorín*) handle.

Sandpaper.

Glue, cola, and water.

A paint brush.

Chapapote, a mixture of tar and gasoline.

Wood. Domingo Galván used *colorín* (*Erythrina Americana, Leguminosa*). Sometimes called *Tzonpantli* (the Aztec name), this is a smooth soft wood with little discernible grain. It is also used to make corks. One source called it the coral bean.

Although *colorín* is the easiest to work with, *palo santo* and occasionally, *sabino* are also used. The more expensive *santos* are made from *sabino. Palo santo* is a tree of tropical America, sometimes called *guaiacum* (*digofilaceas, lignum vitae*). These three woods are used because of their resistance to termites. *Colorín* looks much like pecky cedar. It is pocked by termites but the application of *chapapote* kills them and they do not return.

Palo Santo and the less-used *sabino* are evidently impervious to termites in their natural state and, when carved, they can be successfully protected by *chapapote*. Mexican pine, however, is still a host wood even when painted with *chapapote*. Sr. Galván showed us an 80-year-old *santo* of *colorín* set on a pine base. Although both had been covered with *chapapote*, the pine was honeycombed with the ancient trails of termites while the *santo* itself looked almost new.

It is suggested that the reader use white pine which is easy to work with and, if located in a temperate zone, does not present termite problems as does the pine in more tropical climates. One source suggests the pine be air-dried because if kiln-dried, the wood may become too brittle.

Although balsa is too fragile for this figure, a wood sculptor told me that any wood could be used as long as the carver is aware of its properties.

Because wood is a living thing, you will need to consider the properties of the wood you are using and the particular piece being carved. Because each piece of wood is different, you will not be able to follow the model exactly. It has been said that carving is really releasing a design that has always been there.

Have a sample piece of wood to experiment with. You will need some experience with the tools and it would be desirable if the reader has had some experience in woodcarving. The directions given here are general. The carver worked back and forth between the areas, developing each part more as each area began to take form.

Although the *santero* carved quite a refined Salud (Plate 14 and Figures 1 and 2), it would be possible to stop at about Step 26, at which point Salud is basically formed, or even earlier depending on how refined you want Salud to be. To be a genuine Salud, however, the figure should have a moon.

Sr. Galván's most skilled *santero* was not at the *taller* the day we visited. He had just returned from a twelve-day pilgrimage to the Basilica of Guadalupe and was recuperating. Our *santero* was Serafín León, 18, a skilled craftsman but not as experienced as the recuperating craftsman. He had been woodcarving for only two years.

Carving in the traditional style, Serafín made Salud in six hours —cutting, carving, refining, and staining her.

The cost of Salud, or any saint of *colorín*, is one peso per *cen-*

FIGURE 1

FIGURE 2

tímetro. For *palo santo* it is 5 pesos. This is an extremely low price and does not take into consideration the work involved.

MEASUREMENTS

Salud is one solid, sculptural piece except for part of the world she stands on, the pedestal, and the crescent moon which is attached to the hem of her skirt. Although the measurements of the *santa* are not critical, the proportions are (Figure 3). This Salud is 8½ by 8½ inches: a triangle. The arms follow the same contour as the hair in back and on the sides at a point which is half her length. In front, the sides of her cape and the skirt between are divided into three equal parts gradually becoming wider toward the bottom.

At the widest part, around the raised arms and the flowing hair, Salud is a little over 2½ inches thick. Her narrowest part, around the neck and hair, is 1½ inches thick. Her cape is narrowest at the extended sides which are 1 inch thick. In profile Salud varies between 2 and 2½ inches in thickness. The fold beneath the cape sweeps up 1½ inches to the base of the figure—actually, the top of the world on which she stands. The bottom of the skirt is cut in ½ inch to make the top part of the world. The cape angles up three inches from the base of Salud, one-third her length.

The moon is 4 inches from peak to peak, half the length and width of Salud. As one looks at it, the moon's widest part, the center, is 1 inch from top to bottom. It angles up 2½ inches on each side.

The pedestal is 3 by 3 inches, standing 1 inch high. The bottom of the flattened world, the top part of this piece of wood, is about ¾ inch high. Its diameter is 3 inches.

PROCEDURE

1. Working in the narrow passageway of the patio, Serafín begins with a halved trunk of *colorín*, 9 by 9 by 5 inches. He marks a triangle on it, using a board as his guide. Then he saws the triangle which is Salud's basic form.

2. He chops off the points of the triangle with a *machete* (Figure 4).

3. Then he chops down and rounds off the front surface of the triangle (Figure 5). He will do the back later.

Serafín follows a plaster of paris mold of Salud hanging on the wall although it serves only as a visual guide (see Figure 11).

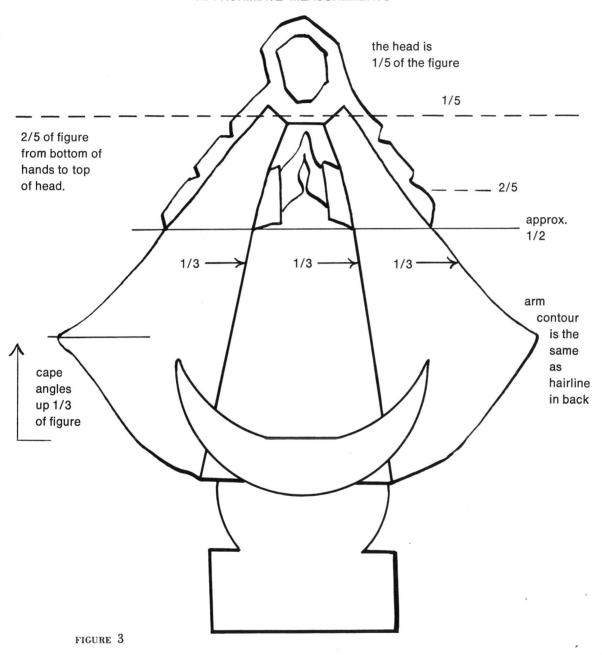

APPROXIMATE MEASUREMENTS

the head is
1/5 of the figure

1/5

2/5 of figure
from bottom of
hands to top
of head.

2/5

approx.
1/2

1/3 →   1/3 →   1/3 →

arm
contour
is the
same
as
hairline
in back

cape
angles
up 1/3
of figure

FIGURE 3

FIGURE 4

FIGURE 5

FIGURE 6

FIGURE 7

FIGURE 8

FIGURE 9

4. Using the twisted file with the chisel ends, he cuts the front lower sides for the wide cape (Figure 6). There are several cracks in the wood, but some will disappear as Serafín carves.

5. Next he cuts in the chin and makes the contours of the face. (Figure 7).

6. About one-third of the way down, he carves in under what will become the configuration of Salud's arms in prayer (Figure 8).

7. He carves more away from the cape.

8. Then he delineates the lines on each side between the skirt and the cape (Figure 9). The central triangular base area where the moon will go later is left alone.

9. In the preceding steps the wood is cut down bit by bit with the large chisel. Serafín used the small chisel very little: for carving the face, for the wrists and the hands, and for the grooves in Salud's hair. He cuts the front hairline of Salud so it comes halfway down the side of her cape.

10. Next he carves a bit more on the cape, the skirt, the area between the face and the raised arms, and the chin line. He delineates her face a little more as well.

11. Then he cuts the top hairline and forms it by cutting in and chipping out. The hair at the cheekline is carved, and then the sides of the folded arms and the hair on the side of the figure are rounded out (Figure 10).

12. Now Serafín delineates the hairline further and smooths the top of the face by carving up toward the hairline. Then to the skirt and to the arms.

13. He continues to round the hair and cuts the skirt in more.

14. He rounds the sides of the wide cape and the sides of the hair.

Serafín continues to follow the mold of Salud on the wall, looking up after every few cuts and studying her form (Figure 11). He follows her pattern generally; his Salud and the prototype will not be exactly alike. No two *santos* are ever exactly alike.

FIGURE 10

FIGURE 11

FIGURE 12

FIGURE 13

15. After all this work, Serafín takes the *machete* and chops some of the back of Salud away (see Figure 12). Until this point, the back of the wood had not yet been touched and was still rough. Although Serafín whacked away confidently, I would advise more careful cutting.

16. In front he makes a slightly curved cut at the bottom of Salud's cape (Figure 12). The wood beneath the cut will be part of the world. He cuts in and chips out.

17. He begins to mold Salud's back by cutting in the hairline which curves across her back, halfway down her cape (Figure 13). Cut in and chip out.

18. Now he cuts in under the bottom sides of her cape, making a deep fold (Figure 14).

SANTO

193

FIGURE 14

Serafín has worked 2½ hours so far.

19. Still using the large chisel, he carves her hair more on the sides, rounds her head, and cuts in further at the back.

20. In the back of the cape, he carves two folds, one on each side. This step is not necessary for the traditional Salud, but it was in this case because one side of this particular piece of wood had a deep depression (see Figure 15). Serafín made the folds to accommodate the wood and balance the figure.

CRAFTS OF
MEXICO

FIGURE 15

21. He carves in all the way around the hair and starts to make three depressions that will delineate her wavy hair (Figure 15).

22. Now Serafín cuts out the center of the cape which leaves a border (Figure 16). The cape is not bordered in back.

23. Using the small chisel, he begins to carve her face which is a raised plane. He carves from the center up and from the center down.

24. He carves her chin more (Figure 17) and then puts three large waves in her hair.

25. Now he grooves the hair with the small chisel. The various grooves, which are $\frac{1}{2}$ to $\frac{1}{4}$ inch long and slightly curved, are not continuous (Figure 18). They only suggest hair. He worked from the top of the hair to the bottom. Serafín later redid all these grooves; he said he had not carved down the head enough.

26. With the small chisel he shapes her wrists and hands and the area between her hands by making three grooves (Figure 19 and following figures). At this point or any previous step, when the figure looks complete enough to you, the carving can be stopped. I have seen pleasing Saluds that are not so refined as this one. But, please add the moon (Steps 28 and 29).

FIGURE 16

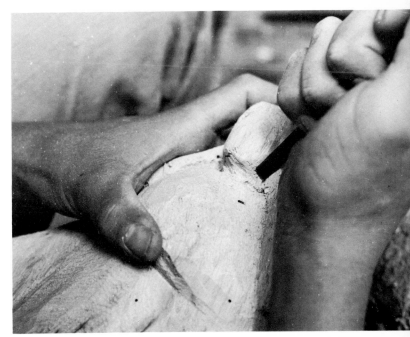

FIGURE 17

FIGURE 18

FIGURE 19

27. To carve the features of Salud's face see Figures 20, 21, and 22. Serafín uses no pencil—he just carves. (Refer to Figure 23 and the following directions).

a. First he delineates the nose by making two vertical grooves and one horizontal groove beneath.

b. For the bottom eyelids, he makes two horizontal lines out from the top of the parallel nose grooves.

c. He chips the wood away from the areas under the eyelines and the horizontal nose line.

d. Then he delineates the mouth—a short line.

e. Now he carves under the cheek line, up from the mouth. Occasionally, when it is necessary for tightly controlled carving, Serafín uses his left thumb to steady the chisel and to apply slight pressure.

f. The eyes are next. Since the bottom lid has already been outlined, he now does the top of the eye, cutting it in more than the bottom lid.

g. He carves the mouth by cutting away from the center line each way, up and down.

FIGURE 20

FIGURE 21

FIGURE 22

FIGURE 23

h. He carves the eyeball between the eyelines and refines the chin a little more. All the facial features have been carved with the small chisel.

28. *La luna*, the moon and *el mundo*, the world, are next.

The moon is cut from a slice of *colorín* branch 3 by 5 by 1 inches. It is first cut into the shape of a half octagon into which a wide V is sliced with lateral ends across the top (Figure 24). He rounds off the moon by chipping the wood with the large chisel (Figure 25). Then he rounds off the edges. It looks terribly large in relation to the small Salud, but that is the custom.

29. For the world, Serafín measures a separate slice of wood against the bottom of Salud. A slice 2 by 3 by 3 inches forms both the bottom half of the world and the pedestal (see Figure 24). He uses a small cut-off saw and cuts into the disc (Figures 26 and 27). How far you cut in depends on the size of your wood. He matches the base of Salud to this disc which will be the bottom part of the world.

Serafín continues to follow the model by eye. There is still no measuring, only matching; no patterns, only looking. He cuts the top and the bottom to match, but starts with the bottom piece. Keep the proportions in mind.

FIGURE 24

FIGURE 25

FIGURE **26**

FIGURE **27**

30. He saws off the rough bottom of the base and begins to carve a slightly convex form. Be sure to carve correctly. The pieces must match and they must be convex—the shape of the world. This seems a hard way to do it, but the world must be done in two parts because of the configuration of Salud's undercape as it flows into the top part of the world. This too is custom.

31. Now he carves the world in further under the flowing cape so it is a single curve (see Figures 2 and 14).

32. He saws down the sides of the cylinder to make it square. This is the pedestal. Then he chips with the large chisel to straighten out the sides, to even and smooth them. It is a flattened world (Figure 28).

SANTO

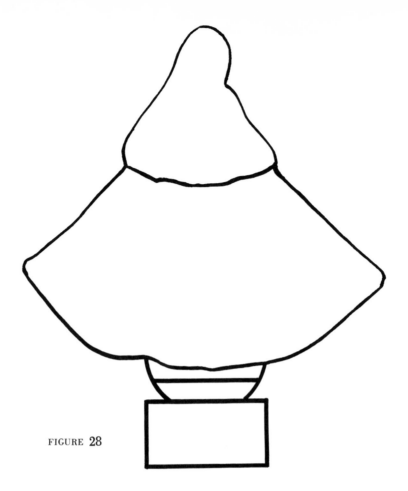

FIGURE 28

33. Now he holds the two parts of the world together and does the final matching with the large chisel. The pedestal has bark impregnated in it. He removes part of it leaving a not unpleasant fault. The bottom of Salud's skirt is still cracked in two places. These cracks are too deep to be removed by carving, but this does not seem to disturb anyone.

34. With a regular, coarse rounded file, Serafín files all around the exposed world, under Salud's cape, and around the joint of the two parts of the world.

35. Because there was no *lija* or sandpaper, at the *taller*, we bought some so Serafín could finish. With the *lija*, he sanded all of Salud except the skirt area where the moon would later be placed. Sanding is easy and fast with this soft wood.

36. He sanded the face very carefully using the now well-worn sandpaper because he had only one grade to use. When sanded, the

grain of the *colorín* showed up only in the moon and on the skirt and cape.

37. This piece of *colorín* did not give when pressed in with the thumb; it was hard and did not need a filler. When the *colorín* does need a filling, *agua fuerte*, a mixture of water and *cola* (glue) is used to fill the wood and strengthen it.

38. Because we could not wait two hours more for the glue to dry, Serafín attached the world and the moon with *clavos*, nails, and then added the glue. The nails were much larger than they needed to be. He hammered down their heads so he could use each end to attach the pieces. Nails are not usually used because the glue is stronger and more certain.

The glue was a crystallized *cola*, usually a fish mucilage; it is sometimes a gelatinous form of animal debris, dried, and bought at the local *tlapalería*, a kind of hardware store. Adding a little at a time, Serafín mixed it with water and heated it in a large tin can on two bricks. A fire of wood shavings (from the carving) and *zacate* (dried grass) was started under the can with kerosene. After stirring the mixture with a wooden stick until it thickened, he inserted the glue with the same stick—dollops of it—between Salud and the moon, and then between the two parts of the world, holding the pieces together by hand for a minute or two.

39. With a large commercial paint brush, he paints on the *chapapote*, a thin mixture of tar and gasoline. This mixture not only stains the *santo* making it look old, but it prevents infestation by termites.

40. When a figure is painted, regular commercial semi-gloss enamel is used and gold leaf is often applied. You may wish to paint Salud. Though I do not know if these colors are traditional, the combination of colors with which the plaster of paris prototype was painted are certainly Mexican. The prototype Salud wore a red dress with green and gold flowers on it. (Salud often has carved flowers on her robe and dress). The model's cape was aqua edged in gold leaf and painted with gold flowers. The underside was dark blue. Her face was white (though the Indians call her the dark Virgin), and her hair was black. She stood on a dark yellow world that sat upon a green pedestal. Unfortunately, the moon had fallen off.

41. If the *santo* is antiqued after it has been painted, *chapapote* is used. In the *chapapote*, gasoline is mixed with the tar instead of kerosene because it dries more quickly and because kerosene can soften the paint beneath. When the *chapapote* is dry, the *santo* is rubbed

with dry cement. Sr. Galván says it takes much experience to do a good antiquing job.

Sr. Galván had an interesting thought about the use of the tar in the *chapapote*. "The tar," he said, "came from the trees of ages ago. It is used with the trees of today. So it is all one. It is all wood. They belong together—the new and the old. It is just a theory, but a very beautiful one, don't you think?"

THE LACQUER OF URUAPAN 14

The earth has its secrets and the mysterious properties of Michoacán's ancient volcanic earth are partly responsible for one of Mexico's oldest, most durable, and most celebrated crafts—the incomparable lacquerware of Uruapan.

The art of *laca* has existed for centuries in Mexico and the middle Americas. Its ingredients are indigenous to the land. Once it was said that the Chinese brought this technique to Mexico. In fact, some of Michoacán's early lacquerware did have graceful oriental scenes of willowy bending trees not known to Mexico. Recent archaelogical findings, however, have disproved this myth. Perhaps the Chinese came to Mexico, but the art of lacquer was already known there. Mexico's lacquers were always lighter and brighter than China's. They had a certain disciplined gaudiness.

Centuries ago Mayan temples in the jungles of Yucatán were vividly lacquered; traces of their color remain to this day. Ancient *al fresco* ceramics are now thought to have been lacquered. But in each case, the organic materials oxidized long ago leaving only the pigment—the color we see today. *Jícaras* with seasoned rinds of gourd incised and lacquered in geometric patterns are listed in the Mendocino Codex as part of tribute paid to the mighty Aztecs.

Lacquered masks have been found in the *yacatas* of the pre-Conquest temples of Michoacán (see Chapter 6). They are thought to have been made in ancient times. And some say even onyx, that smooth semi-precious stone, was once treated with the brilliant, hard lacquers of Mexico.

After the Conquest, the Indians fled the regions of Michoacán and the art of lacquering declined. Then the indefatigable Don Vasco arrived and assigned certain crafts to particular towns (see Chapter 6). He designated Peribán as the center for lacquer crafts. *Peribanas*, or *bateas*, the round, slightly concave lacquered trays, are collector's items and museum pieces today.

Lacquerwork is no longer done in Peribán. Uruapan took over the art long ago as did Pátzcuaro (although in a different style) and Quiroga. Uruapan, however, is today considered the center of Mexico's —and the Americas'—lacquerware.

In the old days the *bateas* from Peribán and from the States of Guanajuato and Jalisco had enormous dimensions. Some were 150 or more *centímetros* wide. Today they are available either new or old for as much as $400 to $800. It is not an inexpensive craft, but neither is the cost equal to the work each piece requires. The model in Plate 15 is 15½ inches in diameter. It took one month to make and it costs $30.

The Spanish changed the art of lacquering only by adding to the number of colors used, and to the number and kinds of objects made. Litters made for saints and religious objects were lacquered as were free-standing closets, commodes, and sewing boxes. The pre-Conquest Indians had had no need for these objects.

The lacquer of Uruapan is incised, inlaid with color, incised again, and then inlaid and rubbed with another color. It requires coats and coats of lacquer and hours of rubbing and polishing each successive color. The technique called *incrustado*, involves a fine inlay of lacquer; it is the method of Uruapan.

Twenty-five years ago, in the *barrio* of Uruapan called San Pedro, whole families engaged in making lacquerware. The people were extremely poor but still they produced the most authentic ware. Working on their front porches, one family member prepared the color and the *tepushta*; another prepared the oil and the *aje*. The most experienced did the actual lacquering and drew the patterns. Little by little the children learned the craft. The skillful movements with which they learned to apply the lacquer became second nature. These ancient skills have been taught for generations.

There are few authentic lacquerware craftsmen today, however. Most people have gone into more lucrative work. The others who still produce lacquerware often take short cuts and do not make the old ware in the old way. "Near the center of town, you will find the men using blowguns and automotive paint to make the *bateas*," said Esperanza Hernandez. "Others will show you the props, such as the *aje*, that rare oil of the insect—but not use them." Esperanza Hernandez says she is one of the two women in Uruapan who still lacquers authentically. "My grandmother's mother did this work. Now, only my sister and I do. My sister's children are not interested in the *laca*. So we are probably the last of our family to do the lacquering."

Esperanza Hernandez lives in a neat mestizo-style house. Scarlet bougainvillea covers the walls and in her large garden, gigantic *noche buena* (poinsettia) trees grow.

"It is fortunate you came now," she said. "If you had come almost any other time, you would have had to stay a few weeks to watch me make one *batea*." Sanded and unsanded *bateas*, some half-lacquered, others partly incised in greens, reds, and blues gleamed on Esperanza Hernandez' covered patio. The Banco Fomento had sent a picture of the old Moon and the Universe pattern to her asking if she would reproduce it. She and her sister were making 100 *bateas* in this design. "That is what we are doing now. The reason we have so many in different stages is that it becomes too boring always doing this same pattern, so we work on different stages at the same time." Because examples of the different stages were all around us, we did not have to wait throughout the month long period of time it normally takes to make a *batea*.

Srta. Hernandez had begun a few weeks earlier. She was not sure how long it would take them to make so many. It was August when we were there. She guessed they might be finished by Christmas or perhaps by January.

When asked about the design, Esperanza replied, "It is old. The crescent moon is Moorish, but it is pre-Conquest, too—*muy antigua*. The flowers and the vines are colonial in detail, but the Mexicans have always loved flowers. The ancient *bateas* were also of the flowers and the plants."

The pattern of the model is the Moon and the Universe done in yellow, white, green, light blue, and black on a background of brilliant red (Plate 15). It is an intricate design with shading and tiny white decorative lines called profiling. Its minute detail is indicative of the late colonial period.

To understand the colors of the Uruapan lacquerware, one must visualize the colorful countryside. In the semi-tropical mountains and meadows, oranges, bananas, chirimoya, and granaditos grow along with massive philodendron and orchards of peach, apricot, and exotic trees. On the mountain peaks grow thick forests of larch, cedar, and oak. Towering pines shade the country roads.

Although the old patterns are still copied, the lacquer patterns have changed over the years. The Tarascan designs were often black with bright flowers, or stylized animals, or plants. Black backgrounds with red, green, blue, or yellow were the most traditional. In colonial days any design was used; they ranged from heraldic designs of Spanish kings and Holy Roman emperors, to dogs standing in the center of large plates enlaced with lacquered flowers. The scenes varied from the mythological to the idyllic pastoral. As the years went by, the designs became more intricate and more baroque, but the graceful ease with which the patterns were applied to the *bateas*—despite their intricacy—was and still is outstanding characteristic of the Mexican lacquer.

In the seventeenth century the figures were smaller. One old *batea* shows an Indian girl, her long braids enveloping her tiaraed head. A small, seed-like yellow and black flower on a background of red was popular in the eighteenth century. This pattern is still being used today. By the mid-nineteenth century, stiff naturalistic flowers and bouquets were lacquered; these were the roses and peonies of Victorian days. The wild orchids of Uruapan and the yellow bulls, sometimes spotted black, were favorites of the 1930's, but in the 1940's, the sentimental rose took over again.

Today one can find both high and low quality lacquerware in Uruapan and in other towns throughout the country. The best work is done by hand using the old techniques and the old motifs. Among the worst work must be a realistic lacquer portrait of President John F. Kennedy surrounded by small, red Michoacán flowers which we saw on one *batea*. The skill it took to do such a work is formidable, but that skill does not insure good design.

Techniques and styles differ from town to town. In Pátzcuaro where the lacquer is brushed on, the craftmen make elaborate, gold-leafed lacquerware. This method was revived several years ago by the craftsman-teacher, Salvador Solchaga, who had remembered how it was done. The work of Pátzcuaro is noted for its delicate brush strokes.

Although Quiroga's style is the most rustic, it is nevertheless still historically authentic. Quiroga has always used a rougher wood and simply painted on their lacquer in a technique called *aplicado*. The familiar black *batea* with red-lacquered flowers is an old design.

In the museum at Morelia, the capital of Michoacán, old *Peribanas* and historical *bateas*—some over 200 years old—are beginning to crackle and craze. Esperanza Cerda makes copies of them; she is one of the Cerda family that pioneered the revival of the crafts of Michoacán in the 1930's.

There is still another center of Mexico's lacquerware. In inaccessible Olinalá, in the State of Guerrero, the craftsmen apply a fine lacquer above which a contrasting color is added. The top color is then incised, revealing the color beneath. It looks like a kind of cloisonné. Chests and boxes from Olinalá are highly prized. The aromatic wood called Olinalau contains a natural jasmine-lemon essence that does not fade with time.

The lacquerware of Mexico is an enigma. Although it looks like a simple process to lacquer a *batea*, it is not. I tried to reproduce what I saw with no success. The materials are peculiar to each region. I suspect the precise ingredients, the exact mixing, and the correct preparation and application of the lacquer are crucial. The craftsman knows his materials only by their common names; he knows how they work, but he does not always know exactly what they are.

Esperanza Hernandez still uses the earth colors. They are brought to her by the Indians of Huétamo, a town in the nearby mountains and a traditional source of material. "Black is the most traditional base color," said Esperanza Hernandez. "White is the hardest to use. It yellows with age."

Patzícua, an altered volcanic glass (obsidian), was once commonly used in the black lacquer. *Iguetacua*, another altered volcanic glass, is used in the white lacquers and with other colors such as red or rose to make them more intense. *Charanda*, a lacquer used on the underside of the *bateas* and the inside of the *jícaras*, is a red earth, an "Indian red" which is gathered from La Charanda, a red hill near the town of Uruapan. All these materials came from the depths of the earth of Michoacán. Expelled from the mouths of the country's seething volcanos, they have lain for years on the surface of the land.

The wood, or *aile*, for the trays is brought to Señorita Hernandez by the Indians from the mountain pueblos of Tingambato and Tancítaro. As it is only roughly carved, she sends it to a local carpenter to be sanded. "He can smooth it better than I can with his machine," she said. "But once the craftsman had to spend many hours sanding these *bateas* himself."

But what are *aile* and *Tzirimu*, the other traditional wood used for the lacquer? In Mexico, it is often difficult and sometimes impossible to find the generic name of a plant. For each wood there are local names, Spanish names, and Indian names. One plant may have fifteen acceptable names. Although a few have tried heroically to identify the plants of Mexico (some in extensive studies), no one has succeeded in finding them all.

Tzirimu, a very white, grainless wood also called by its Spanish name, *sirimo*, is the linden tree of the family of the birch. *Aile* is an alder of the genus *aldus*, the Spanish name of which is *aliso*. It is also a tree of the birch family. These historical woods have little resin so they readily absorb the oils used in the lacquer.

Pine has been used in poorer pieces, but it is unsuited to this medium because it is resinous. The resin, seeking a surface, can cause the lacquer to explode and crackle. Some sources, however, claim that an extremely resinous pine is used. Señorita Cerda of Morelia summed it up very well when she said, "Well, if you want to lacquer a *batea* just for the experience, use pine. It may last a month, it may last years. But you will never know until you try and then it will be too late."

The size, or *sisa*, is the basis of the lacquer. It contains three elements: the *tepushta*, the *aje*, and the oil (coloring is not part of the size).

The *tepushta*, a gray-white, hard earth, is said to come from ancient, secret quarries in the mountains near Uruapan. It is dolomite, a calcium calcareous, magnesium silicate that resists water and heat as does the lacquer of Uruapan. *Tepushta* can be used to make cement.

At least three elements of the lacquer are glass: they are the *patzícua*, the *iguetacua*, and the *charanda*. Perhaps it is these altered volcanic glasses mixed with the durable natural *tepushta* that produces the shiny, hard surface of the lacquer.

Maque is the term used for the size after the color is added, polished, and dried. Since the procedure is done by hand, this method of lacquering in Mexico is called *maque a mano—maque* by hand.

The *sisa* and the colors must be ground to dust. Grinding color was a common task in ancient Mexico and women often spent two days grinding one color for their *laca*.

The second part of the *sisa* is the oil. The oil of the *chia* seed was once used; each tiny seed was toasted and ground. Before that, the *chicalote* seed was gathered. Today everyone uses *linaza,* the common, commercial linseed oil which is boiled over a slow fire for several minutes (everyone gave a different length of time) until it thickens to a sticky, brown substance. Some say a sliver of *ocote* should be added to the simmering oil. "But this is not necessary," said Esperanza Hernandez.

The third ingredient, the most important and the greatest problem to the reader who might wish to try lacquering, is the *aje.* *Aje* (*cocus axin*) is an insect which, as far as I can discover, is found only in Mexico. *Aje* is also the name of an oily substance produced from the insect. Without it the Mexican lacquer would probably not exist, for this is the base of the lacquer. Oil alone is a slow drying agent. It would be impossible to effect this glossy hard surface without a good, quick drying agent of some kind.

Srta. Hernandez buys her *aje* already prepared from the Indians of Huétamo, the traditional source of the *aje* as well as the colors. To make it, the Indians place the insects in cornhusks filled with cornsilk. Stored in a dry place for the winter, they spin a cocoon. These bundles are then tied to a tree, the cocoons hatch, and a new batch of *aje* is propagated on the tree where it dutifully stays until it is scraped off and prepared for the lacquer workers.

The *aje* is washed and then boiled in water until it disintegrates. When the wax flows to the surface, the solution is strained through a cloth and put into jars to stand for twenty hours or so. After it is slightly coagulated, it is stirred until small balls form. These are put over a slow fire to remove the moisture. Afterward the wax is strained and cooled. Then it is ready to be used.

The *aje* is now a dark orange substance that smells a little like rancid butter. Wrapped in cornhusks again, looking like a fat tamale, it is brought to town.

Aje was cultivated centuries ago in Mexico, but some sources still insist that sumac was used. Sumac, however, does not grow in Mexico but in China, where they do use it for their lacquers.

If one does not have *aje,* it is said that one can use red oxide of lead, oxide of manganese, acetate of lead, litharge, garlic, onion, and even bread. This, however, is hearsay!

The lacquer making of Mexico is a highly refined process comprising many subsidiary processes just as intricate and just as precise. It is one of the most unusual crafts of Mexico and certainly one of the most complicated but without it, no book on Mexican crafts could really be complete. The story of the lacquer is a story of the ingenuity of the Mexican craftsman.

Working with the Craftsman

TOOLS AND MATERIALS

A bowl of linaza.

Aje.

Dolomite or tepushta.

A smooth wooden tray.

A rayador, a sharp steel knife of the type used for cutting mat. (Once this graver was a thorn of maguey.)

Cloth for the lap.

Small cloths, one for each color (some say cotton can be used instead).

PROCEDURE

1. The rough *batea* (Figure 1) must be sanded to an extremely smooth surface.

2. Srta. Hernandez puts her fingers in the *linaza* (into which the *aje* has been melted) and rubs it over the surface of the top of the *batea*, quickly and lightly (Figure 2). Her movements are skillful and swift.

3. The *dolomia* and the pigment, which are both as fine as dust, are mixed together. She picks up this powdered, red pigment mixture with her fingers and smooths the color on the *batea* with the heel of her hand (Figure 3). Again, her movements are rapid. This deftness and quickness is necessary if the color—and later, the design—is not to become blurred or dulled.

4. Now she dips a cloth into more of the dry pigment and *dolomia* mixture and "dusts" it over the entire surface. This, too, is done rapidly and lightly (Figures 4 and 5).

If any part of the lacquered surface begins to dry before it is

CRAFTS OF
MEXICO

210

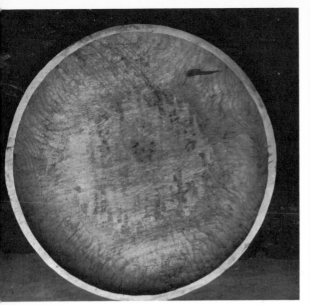

FIGURE 1 FIGURE 2

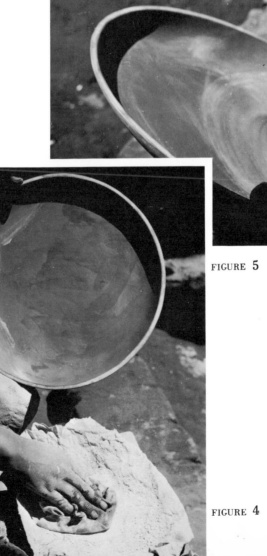

FIGURE 5

FIGURE 3

FIGURE 4

polished, she keeps it moist by applying more oil and *aje*. Then she polishes the area with a dry cloth (Figure 6).

In other words, *oil* the area, *rub* in the pigment (but not too hard), *dust* it with the powdered pigment on a cloth, then *polish* with a dry cloth. These steps are repeated six times, one right after the other.

5. After the six coats are applied, the *batea* is set aside to dry for three or four days. To apply the basic lacquer coats of red, it has taken Esperanza Hernandez only a half hour.

6. After three or four days, she cuts the design with the *rayador*, the strong steel graver (Figure 7). Srta. Hernandez does not draw her design first (although the reader should). She memorized her designs long ago. Though her sister works with her, Esperanza does all the drawing. The lacquer, still not hard, has a consistency like that of thick plastic ribbon, and it remains flexible allowing the fine cutting necessary to make the design. All the incising is cut through this base coat of lacquer to the wood, although the wood itself is not cut.

7. Srta. Hernandez incises the pattern *for one color at a time, from dark to light*. She cuts the black areas first (Figure 8) using a clean cloth to wipe away the "dust." (She uses a different cloth for each color.) She applies the black pigment in the same way she applied the red base coats. Since the only incised area is black, she does not worry about going over the edges; it will come off naturally when the pigment is rubbed on with the cloth. The black is applied six times. This brings the filled-in area up to the surface of the red.

The secret of recognizing fine *incrustado* lacquerware is to run your finger over the surface. If you can feel a demarcation between the colors, it is not an example of well-done *incrustado*.

8. The *batea* is again set aside to dry for 3 or 4 days.

9. Now the pattern for the green area is incised. It is applied in the same way as the red and the black and is set aside for 3 or 4 days to dry.

10. Next the pattern for the light blue is incised and inlaid (Figures 9, 10, and 11); the same process is repeated six times and the *batea* is allowed to dry for another 3 or 4 days.

11. The pattern for the yellow is cut and filled in next. The application of the yellow includes the "shading" of yellow in the black leaves.

12. Last, the white is inlaid and the intricate profiling is done. The profiling or the incision of fine lines is precision work. It must be lacquered the same way as the rest of the *batea*.

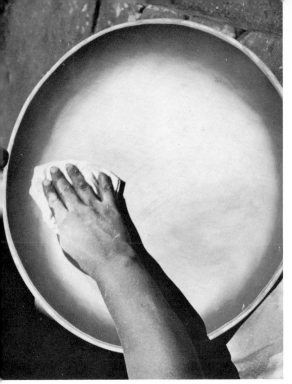

FIGURE 7

FIGURE 6

FIGURE 9

FIGURE 8

FIGURE 10

FIGURE 11   FIGURE 12

13. The *batea*, its design completed, is set aside to dry.

14. The underside of the *batea* is lacquered with the *charanda*. (This is usually done only on the finer pieces.) The entire undersurface is lacquered six times in the same way the base coats of lacquer were applied.

15. Now the rim is lacquered six times and dried for 3 or 4 days. Both the rim and the underside are done last because they are handled the most during the earlier work. The surface design, done first, is protected by its concave form.

16. Finally, a clean rag is dipped in *linaza* with a small amount of fine abrasive and the complete *batea* is polished. Esperanza Hernandez simply calls this abrasive *tierra*—earth. The tiny particles of earth in the oil shine and clean away any extra paint that may be left where it should not be.

Because of the need to wait for the pigment and the *sisa* to dry between colors it takes at least one month to lacquer these authentic *bateas*. At the "automotive" shops where synthetic paints are used, a *batea* can be finished in a matter of hours. These "automotive *bateas*" will be stronger, but they are not the real *bateas* of ancient Mexico whose lacquer has been called the original plastic because of its strength, durability, and gloss.

PART

VI

PAPER

MASKS OF CELAYA 15

We arrived in Celaya on the eve of its quatricentennial, the 400th anniversary of the city's founding. Once an old Spanish city, today Celaya is a booming town in the Bajio. Within the last fifteen years, wide paved boulevards have replaced the dirt roads and modern factories, office buildings, and residences have been constructed.

With industrialization, Celaya is losing its beauty. It is not as picturesque as the guide books say. For instance, it is the city where the residents of San Miguel go to buy automotive parts and refrigerators. The Celayanses go to San Miguel, Querétaro, or Guanajuato for their old world charm. Two signs announce the population: one says 80,000, another 140,000—the latter is more accurate.

The streets of Celaya are busy. We pass trucks loaded with tomatoes and corn and men carrying sacks of grain. Bundles of flour and piles of bricks are stacked on the sidewalk. Women carry baskets to market; men carry firewood. Sidewalk vendors line the narrow streets while small trucks and tractors lumber by. We see a huge basket eight feet high, being readied for the parade tomorrow. Brandy barrels draped with plastic grape leaves sit on a trailer which will also be in the parade. The busy streets are clogged with cars, trucks, buses, pedestrians, and vendors.

Then we pass the old plaza where perfectly clipped laurel trees form a continuous square. Within the square is a continuous circle of more laurel. Not much is left of the elegant old city, but as compensation, the blocks of once-dismal square-fronted houses have had their fronts repainted by a city decree. These modest newly painted homes with one door and one window, or perhaps no window, form a vibrant array of color—a bright purple next to a bright blue, a doorway of red with yellow and black diamonds. A green house stands next to a brilliant blue-green. Another is melon pink and one is half yellow and half blue. Next to it is a larger house of carnelian with lavender and pink woodwork and aqua window gratings.

Here are the people who make and buy the masks of Celaya. These are the colors they use. The wild and garish colors of the Celaya mask are not wild and garish to the user. They are colors he has always used.

Past the plaza, we found the place we were looking for. It was not a *taller*, but a warehouse. This is the warehouse of Paulo Chico, one of the three middlemen in Celaya who buy papier-mâché items. He in turn sells the masks and toys all over the country and in various parts of the world.

In the warehouse deep baskets and cardboard boxes held dozens of long, thin devil masks in yellow, purple, and red; all these lacquered masks had red, white, and black striped horns. There were also skeleton masks, some plain black and white (see Plate 16), others with green and red garlands on their heads or with multicolored crowns. Their hollow eyes were rimmed in pink, purple, yellow, and red. A Victorian lady mask and a Maximilian mask were side by side: Maximilian of the white face, the blue eyes, the golden beard—the storybook soldier.

Mickey Mouse, the old fashioned Chinese, foxes, rabbits, a gold-toothed woman face, jaguars, all painted in improbable colors were here. And one blue-rimmed mask looked suspiciously like the Ku Klux Klan. The regular unlacquered masks were 50 centavos, while the lacquered ones were 1 peso. We bought a trunkload which came to 43.50 pesos (about $5).

Papier-mâché burros, goats, and bulls were crowded into one large bin and in another were tiny brooms and dishes, and baskets smaller than a thimble. Papier-mâché hats also abounded: centurions' hats in red, white, and green (the national colors of Mexico) and

Viva Mexico hats for the recent Independence Day.

There were some plastic rattles and a few other cheap plastics, but not many. Most of the masks and toys here were made in the traditional ways in the simple homes of the surrounding area. Some make the masks and toys all year; others augment their income in this way when they cannot work in the fields.

Some craftsmen make little toys of brightly painted tin, others create miniature wooden furniture. There were also the *matracas*, ingenious, movable wooden toys: pull a string or lift a lid and a cowboy lifts his rifle, a horse gallops, a bird sips, or a skeleton jumps.

Papier-mâché horses one foot high sit on platforms with wheels. Small horses' heads are set on bamboo sticks for riding. Birds perch on gourds. Fanciful papier-mâché rattles are attached to sticks as are dolls' heads.

Dolls are made with clay heads and cloth bodies. A few are made from paster of paris. The hussy dolls that look like the hefty circus riders on the posters of 50 years ago are one of the most unusual toys of Celaya and of Mexico. Like the crude but clever *matracas* and the masks, these classic dolls are museum pieces today. The dolls are usually about a foot high but they can be larger. Those made of papier-mâché sell at the factory for 22 pesos per dozen. Their arms and legs are crudely jointed and their faces painted—the eyes are always blue or lavender. An old fashioned bathing suit of a muddy mauve color is painted on and they often wear white knee socks under painted-on pumps. The floral and leaf decoration on the front of the dolls is the only delicate part. Their red or black hair is most often in a pony tail; their skin is dark peachy-pink. Glitter is sprinkled on wet glue for the earrings and necklaces. All have their names prominently printed on their suits: Eloa Cesilia, Olibia [*sic*]. A few wear Nehru hats.

Ignacio López Barrera and Loreto Luna, his wife, make many of these papier-mâché figures as do many others in town. It was Sra. Barrera who made the skeleton mask for us (Figure 9). "We make all the designs," said Loreto Luna. I asked Loreto why her name had the masculine ending (usually the name for a woman would be, Loreta). "I come from San Miguel," she replied. "There is a church there of that name. It is a beautiful church. I am named after it."

At their *taller* we saw boxes of chunky arms and legs waiting to be attached to the cumbersome bodies of the Celaya dolls. In one corner a girl was making *viejito* masks for the famous Michoacán Dance of the Old Men. Near one end of the patio a boy was building a

5-foot papier-mâché church. He used a postcard for his model, though it was the famous Tresguerras church, El Carmen, just a few blocks away. Behind him, a girl was putting the last bit of paper on a four-foot frame of the world. "These are all for floats in the parade tomorrow," said Loreto. Three large butterflies with five-foot wingspans were drying on wire armatures waiting to be painted. They, too, would be part of the parade. "We still have two more to begin," said Loreto. Another girl was painting a large, vermilion crown for one of the papier-mâché queens.

Besides preparing for the parade, the workers were painting the allegorical *alabrijes*, 2 foot high dragons with a witchy medieval look painted in purple, silver, green, and red.

About twenty people worked along the narrow cement patio. The house ran along one side, the well-equipped kitchen on the other. Pots, cans, and pails of flowers hung from the yellow walls. High metal frames standing beneath them held still more flowers. And below these were the large clay bowls filled with the many paints being used.

Besides the imminent parade, the Day of the Dead was coming soon, so two other workers were making large skeleton figures. Stacks of bony bodies, heads, arms, and legs were cast in one corner.

Someone else was painting several large devil masks. "Not to wear," said Loreto. "These are for walls. It is for an order from Mexico City."

Loreto Luna's husband was in Monterey where he had been sent by the government to teach prisoners how to work with papier-mâché. Next he would go to Chihuahua and then perhaps to other areas in the north. "He is teaching them so they will have something to do and to be able to earn a little money while they are in jail."

When we returned the next day all the papier-mâché for the floats was gone. "Did you finish?"

"Of course," said Loreto matter-of-factly. "Now we are getting ready for the Day of the Dead (see Figure 1). Then for Christmas we make St. Joseph and the burro for the crêches, the *nacimientos*." She told us someone else must make the figures of the Virgin Mary and Jesus for they did not. "Corpus Cristi is our biggest time. We make most of our toys for this."

Corpus Cristi, a movable date in late spring, is the time of the miniatures. Children dress up like their elders and carry small replicas of the products their elders make. Thousands of small burros are made for this day as well. It is also the Saint's Day of the Manuels. Loreto

FIGURE 1

made no mention of the Christmas Fair in Celaya where much pottery and papier-mâché is said to be sold.

It is difficult to ascertain when a certain craft actually began; everyone tells you something different. All that is definitely known is that Celaya is one of the old papier-mâché centers in Mexico. No one knows how old.

Jovita Prieto, a 72-year-old toy maker who makes pastel-dappled papier-mâché horses told us that the toy making began when she was a little girl. When her father died, she and her brother had to go to work, so she began to make molds and toys which were sold in Mexico City. She thinks her employers were the first to make them.

The making of masks in Mexico, however, goes back at least as far as 1000 B.C. The present day Yaqui mask, an actual deer's head, is said to go back to antiquity. The jaguar mask of Guerrero is also old. In pre-Conquest Mexico, death masks and votive masks were made of shell, turquoise, obsidian, stone, quartz, jade, gold, and probably other materials. The papier-mâché masks, however, came after the

MASKS OF CELAYA

Conquest, probably much later, for it was the Spanish who introduced the craft of making papier-mâché.

It is thought that the original use of masks was ceremonial. Today they are still used for folk dances, for ceremonies, and also just for fun. The contemporary mask, even when made in a "new" medium such as papier-mâché, is said to retain the ancient tradition, the ancient feeling.

Masks are made in all parts of the country. Some are carved wood and others are woven reed. They are also made of armadillo, or snakeskin, or hide. Those masks made of tin are new, introduced within the last thirty years. Clay masks are found wherever there is clay.

Although genuine teeth and real hair are occasionally incorporated into the masks, wool, dried grasses, fur, or rope are usually used for eyebrows, beards, and other projections.

Papier-mâché masks are made in a few other towns in the Bajio: Querétaro, Irapuato, and Silao. Mexico City and Puebla have a large output as well. But the tradition of papier-mâché is said, generally, to have come from Celaya and it has been called the finest in Mexico. In the small towns of the central plateau, near the plazas, vendors sell these masks for a few centavos. When asked where the masks are from, they will usually say, "Celaya."

Working with the Craftsman

TOOLS AND MATERIALS

Paper. Loreto Luna uses cement bags, the strongest source of paper.

Flour and water paste.

A knife.

A mold. Many of the clay molds of the papier-maché mask makers were made years ago. Because they have been handed down through the families, some traditional masks are seen again and again. The model, a skeleton with a crown, and a grinning, toothy unicorn were just two of the archetypes we saw at the López *taller*.

To make a new mold, plaster of paris is poured over a prototype of pastilene, "but anything can be used for a mold," said Loreto. Her husband, Ignacio López Barrera, makes all their new models.

Animal fat or ceba (*car oil*). Vaseline would work as well.

Three brushes, a thick round brush with short bristles, a small brush to paint the *rayas*, the lines, and a little larger brush to paint in the red-rimmed eyes.

Brushes of squirrel tail are made at the *taller* by cutting the hairs from the tail and binding them to a stick with a thick, tight band of thread. The squirrel skins are brought in by hunters.

Blanco de españa (calcium carbonate), the common whiting material used in Mexico. Commercial gesso could be used.

Red and black paint. These are powdered pigments mixed with water and *cola*, the fish mucilage (see Chapter 13). Poster paints could be used.

The paint is mixed to a thick consistency in large clay bowls. Yellow, green, shocking pink—all the colors are lined up along the patio wall waiting to be used on the various papier-mâché fantasies.

MEASUREMENTS

Measuring straight across the back of the skeleton mask, it is 7 inches long (not counting the $2\frac{3}{4}$-inch area that goes straight back under the chin), $5\frac{1}{4}$ inches across the widest area, just above the eyebrows, and 4 inches across the narrowest area, the center of the mouth. The convexity is roughly 3 inches according to the contours of the face. The dome of the forehead and the tip of the nose are $3\frac{1}{2}$ inches; the cheekbones, 3 inches; the eye sockets begin at 2 inches on the side and angle up slightly toward the bridge of the nose. The convexity to the center of the mouth is $2\frac{1}{4}$ inches, and the point of the chin juts out to $2\frac{3}{4}$ inches.

PROPORTIONS

Divide the face of the mask into four equal parts horizontally (see Figure 2). The first two parts are the forehead. The painted crossbar of the forehead cross marks the point between the first and second parts. The third part extends from the bridge of the nose to the top lip and the fourth part, from the top lip to the point of the chin. The eyes are halfway between the second and third parts and the ears are in the second and third parts. The cheekbones are little mounds between the eyes and the mouth; the triangularly shaped nose is placed between the eyes and the cheekbones.

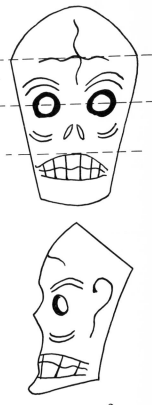

FIGURE 2

PROCEDURE

1. Working in her patio, Loreto Luna makes a thick paste of flour and water. She mixes it in a tin can and places it on two bricks over a fire. She boils it "just a little."

2. She sometimes covers the mold with animal fat so that the paper will not stick, but she does not always lubricate the old molds. These dark clay molds glisten from years of oil saturation and probably don't need further lubrication. The reader, however, should use some kind of oil.

3. Working on her knees before a slightly raised, wide platform of wood covered with gunny sack, she takes one layer of the brown paper (cement bag), about 30 by 25 inches, and rubs the paste freely over both sides with her hands.

4. She doubles this paper, adds more paste to each outer side, and then she squeezes it into a ball working the paste through the paper.

5. Spreading out the sticky paper, she tears a 2-inch-wide strip the length of the paper. She folds this strip lengthwise and flattens it while she adds more paste to each outer side. She places the *folded* edge of this strip around the perimeter of the mask mold (Figures 3 and 4) where it serves to reinforce the vulnerable edges. If necessary, she tears more strips and repeats the process.

6. Now she tears a 4-by-4-inch piece from the large section of paper, rubs it again on each side with the paste, and applies it to the mold. She does this several times until the surface of the mold is covered. She also covers the eye sockets.

7. She applies two layers, putting on the second without waiting for the first to dry. Except for the edging, the application appears rather haphazard, but it is more important that the papier-mâché be firmly applied and securely pressed into the contours than that it be neat. Loreto has applied the papier-mâché quickly, covering the mold in a matter of minutes.

8. She sets the mask aside to dry for at least 2 or 3 hours. The drying time will depend upon the weather.

9. After the mask is dry, she lifts it from the mold, using a long knitting needle to separate the mask from the mold around the edges (Figure 5). If it does not come off readily, Loreto splits the mask under the chin to remove it. Then she papier-mâchés the split. This step is not always necessary.

10. Now, using a regular knife, she cuts out the eyes from the front (Figure 6). Any kind of knife will do. Loreto borrowed one from us because she couldn't find hers.

FIGURE 3
FIGURE 4

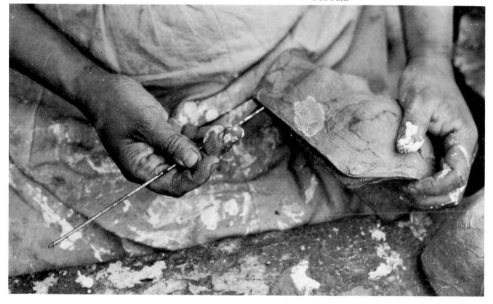

FIGURE 5

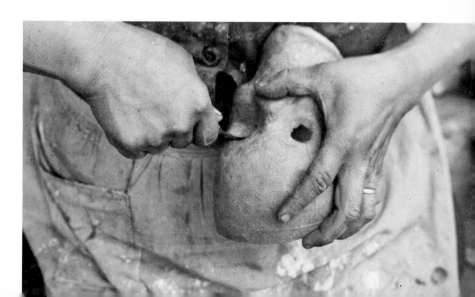

FIGURE 6

FIGURE 8

FIGURE 7

FIGURE 9

11. She applies a thick coat of *blanco de españa* so that she "won't have to put on more than one coat." This whiting is painted on with a thick, round, short-bristled brush (Figure 7). Commercial gesso would work just as well or better.

12. She sets the mask aside to dry for 20 minutes or so.

13. With the smallest brush, she paints the lines on the mask. Beginning with the mouth, she works more or less from the bottom up, one side at a time. First she outlines the complete bottom lip, then the top lip, and then the wavery teeth—following the general impressions of the mask. Next she paints both nostrils, the cheek lines on one side, and one eyebrow and one ear. After completing the other side, she paints the forehead cross (Figure 8).

Occasionally Loreto uses her little finger to steady her hand as she paints, but her hand is naturally steady. She does all the "crucial" finish painting. Yet nothing is really crucial here. It is all a matter of spirit in expression and a "mistake" here and there is of no consequence.

14. She waits a few minutes for the paint to dry.

15. Finally, with a fairly thick brush, Loreto paints in the wide red rim of the skeleton's eyes and he is finished (Plate 16 and Figure 9). The traditional mask is not lacquered.

16 *PAPIER-MÂCHÉ*

A sophisticated form of papier-mâché is made in the town of San Miguel de Allende. The innovators, Jeanne Valentine Schlee, a Parisian by birth, and Guy Schlee, a native Londoner, create a world of elegant papier-mâché products in their factory on Pila Seca Street.

Their work is an example of contemporary foreign influence on the Mexican. While the method is French, one could say the design is Mexican, for it is adapted to the Mexican motifs. The result is a new product.

This is historically significant. The first foreign influence to fuse with and to change the crafts of Mexico was Spanish. The crafts have been changing ever since. Even before the Conquest, new waves of people and possibly early wanderers from all directions brought new ideas and new techniques. One tribe moving in on another changed not only their life style but their arts and crafts as well. The old was altered and new forms were created. This process continues today.

The Valentine papier-mâché factory is in a centuries-old Spanish colonial building, one of many that line the cobblestone streets of this old central Mexican town. Inside, bibelots and fanciful creatures are found in various stages of development (Figure 1). All the work is done by hand. Molds are cast, stencils cut, bare structures created in papier-mâché, decorations applied and deftly painted. In the large

228

interior patio a row of satisfied papier-mâché cats, three feet tall, await shipment to the United States. Other pieces are drying. Fifty people work here, although everything is designed either by Jeanne Valentine or by her son, Nicolas Schlee. They work with light, bright colors that are the distinctive trademark of Jeanne Valentine's work.

Besides a fanciful cortege of creatures, there are decorative boxes of all kinds and sizes, hand mirrors, and mirror frames. There are also countless flowered, starred, or valentined objets d'art in mottled pink, white, turquoise, cocoa, yellow, and orange. The creatures: lions, huge cats with crowns, great filigreed owls, giant Easter egg hens and ducks, parrots, macaws, pious golden-haired angel candelabra, British soldiers waiting to stand at attention over boudoir bottles; gay, lacy Tehuantepec girls holding hands across a papier-mâché bedstand. The wickedly enchanting chess set in red and black has traditional Mexican figures, beribboned and shirred with string, lace, and bright, light color.

Elegant furniture designed and produced here is also papier-mâché antiqued in gold, bronze, white, or any color you might wish. It is decorated with bronzed fruit, flowers, Aztec suns and moons, and animals or birds in subdued colors.

A few fine dresses are still designed and made by Jeanne Valentine. Her draperies, table cloths, bedspreads, and tea sets have the same light touch, appliquéd or embroidered, that gently dominates the papier-mâché. The two arts have come together in the center of San Miguel at the atelier of Jeanne Valentine, S.A., the company which embraces two enterprises—papier-mâché and dress design.

The visitor will find a chess set, a large, impossibly pink burro, a basket of pink and bright blue flowers, and a carousel bar with glass holders around the rim of its canopy. Wrought iron lamps, tables, and candelabra repose gracefully at one end of the shop.

The dresses are on the balcony in the *costurera*. One can try them on in a pink dressing room, guarded by a green-eyed papier-mâché tiger and see how they look in a large mirror framed by a papier-mâché garland of pink and blue flowers.

The papier-mâché enterprise was begun ten years ago and now the products are sold all over Mexico and exported to France, Switzerland, Spain, the United States, and most of the world. Some years before, Gemma Tacogna had begun to make a new kind of papier-mâché in Mexico. Originally from New York, she maintains her studio in Mexico City where she perfects imaginative and rather baroque figures of deep, rich color. Each is well known. Each creates an enchanting, but different world of bewitchery and charm.

As we have said, it was the Spanish who brought paper making, as we know it, to Mexico. They were early craftsmen of papier-mâché, probably having learned the technique from the Asians, who were the first to use it. It is possible that the craft became widespread during the reign of Maximilian, the Austrian who became Mexico's emperor under the direction of the French government. The history of papier-mâché is closely bound to France and though the rule of Maximilian was short, the influence of the French is still felt, particularly in the cities of central Mexico.

Before the Conquest, paper was made from the bark of the *amatl* tree as some bark paintings are today. In the mountains, it is said that this paper is still used for witchcraft and that black magic is practiced with *amatl* paper cut-outs. Another paper, a kind of papyrus, was made from the fiber of the maguey plant. It was on this paper that the Aztecs wrote their pictographic codices and kept records of tribute exacted from their minions. One levy listed in such a record was 8000 reams of paper.

The Valentine technique is more refined than the bold, slightly slapdash method of traditional Mexican papier-mâché (see Chapter 15). Whereas much of Mexican papier-mâché has a dull surface and is generally a coarse looking non-durable product, the Valentine papier-mâché is characterized by a finished look and a surface patina (Plate 17). It is formed over wood or in original handcrafted molds.

In the spirit of the country, a country in which originality, inventiveness, and fantasy prosper, the papier-mâché of Jeanne Valentine thrives. Imagination is limitless. Constantly designing and trying new ideas in whatever they do, their finished product is always delightfully different, a mixture of French and Mexican tradition with a flourish of invention. Their commodity is refined whimsy—an example of a "new" craft of Mexico.

Working with the Craftsman

TOOLS AND MATERIALS

For the mold:

Clay.

Wood (for the box that is put around the prototype).

Pure soap.

Plaster of paris.

For the papier-mâché figure:

Newsprint or old newspapers.

A thin cardboard mat.

Flour and water paste (or wallpaper paste).

Elmer's glue (or another synthetic white medium).

Vaseline (or another kind of grease).

Scissors.

A knife.

A file.

A small stick that is not too sharp.

A long (7-inch) needle with a large eye.

Heavy string.

Brown wrapping paper.

Rope for epaulets and braid.

White latex-base paint or *gesso.*

Ordinary varnish.

A narrow brush.

Imitation silver and gold leaf.

Water-base paints.

Lacquer, spray or liquid. If liquid is used, you will need a three-inch brush and thinner to dilute the lacquer.

For antiquing:

A soft rag.

Black water-base paint.

The measurements of the soldier in Plate 17 (see also Figure 2 and 10) are not included here for he is a complicated figure. You will necessarily have to make your own prototype and mold if you build him. Therefore, I suggest you use him simply as a guide. It is the

FIGURE 1

method that is important if you wish to use papier-mâché in this new but highly individualistic technique of Mexico.

PROCEDURE

Making the Mold

1. The 18-inch soldier in Figure 2 is formed to sit astride a fearless horse. Nicolas Schlee, premier designer, works directly with the clay to produce his ideas. When the clay form is complete, the surface is "polished," or smoothed, then set aside to partially dry for a few days (in the shade). It is not dried "bone hard," but only enough so as not to be destroyed during subsequent careful handling.

2. Now it must be determined where the dividing line on the figure will be drawn, for a plaster of paris mold must be made in two parts. The way in which the resultant mold is pulled free of the clay sculpture determines the position of the line. The clay model is studied to be sure neither section of the mold will have undercuts. The idea of the breakaway mold is to have a mold from which to make replicas of the

FIGURE **2**

original. While the reader may wish to make only one, this is the method used at the Jeanne Valentine atelier. (The mold-making process for papier-mâché is exactly the same as that used in making molds for ceramics. Any manual or craft book that deals with plaster of paris, or with molds, should also give details for this process.)

3. This soldier, the clay model, is divided lengthwise. Looking at his full profile, a line is drawn exactly in the middle of his silhouette from the bottom of his foot on one side, up to his hat, and down the other side to the bottom of his other foot.

4. He is then placed on a smooth wooden platform which forms the bottom of the "box," in which the mold will be formed. The platform determines the size of the mold. (See Figures 3, 4, and 5 to see the relationship between the resultant plaster of paris mold and the size of the figure.)

5. A "box" of flat wooden walls is then built around the soldier. This box, assembled into the required shape, is made of wood or ply strong enough to resist the pressure of the plaster. Thickness and strength vary according to the size of the piece being modelled. It is held together by clamps.

Enough space—usually 1½ inches—is left between the figure and the box to insure that the mold will not break. But neither must the mold be too heavy or bulky. Coat the whole figure with liquid soap.

6. Now soft clay is built up to the dividing line (see Step 2) all around the soldier. In other words, exactly one half of the figure is encased in loosely built-up clay. This clay forms a wall between the figure and the walls of the box, isolating the section to be molded.

7. Plaster of paris is poured around the exposed half of the figure in the box. The plaster takes 10 to 15 minutes to set.

8. When dry, the mold is turned over, the box taken away, and the built-up clay that was on the bottom is removed.

9. The exposed plaster is given a coat of liquid soap so that the next section poured will not adhere to the first.

10. The box is replaced and the other half of the mold is poured.

11. When this side is dry, the box is tapped gently to break the vacuum and to remove the box. The two halves of the plaster of paris mold separate and you now have the two-part mold for the papier-mâché figure.

Making the papier-mâché figure

12. Grease the inside of the plaster of paris mold and be sure no plaster is left unprotected. (Vaseline is a good medium for this.) The mold is now ready for the first layer of paper.

13. The paper may be newsprint or old newspapers torn into 2- to 3-inch squares. The paper should not be cut because the torn edges make a more interesting and softer texture.

14. Flour and water is boiled to a creamy consistency for the first layer of paper. (Wallpaper paste can be used).

15. Using double layers of paper, the paste is applied to both sides of the paper with the fingers and applied to the mold (Figure 3). For the nooks and crannies, the paper is torn into smaller pieces and pushed into them with a small stick (use any kind as long as it is not too sharp). Each layer is allowed to dry before beginning the next.

16. The second layer is then applied using thin cardboard mat, two sheets at a time (Figure 4). From now on instead of the paste, use Resistol (Mexico's Elmer's glue) or some other synthetic medium.

17. The third layer is applied, using newsprint again. Colored comics can be used for this layer, but because the color may seep through, they should never be used for the last layer.

18. When dry, the papier-mâché is gently loosened along the

FIGURE 3

FIGURE 5

FIGURE 4

edges with the fingers and pulled up a little at a time to prevent tearing (Figure 5).

19. Any rough edges are scraped off with the knife.

20. The edges of the two halves are matched, then sewed together with a large needle threaded with heavy string (Figure 6).

21. After sewing, the seam is covered with torn strips of strong, brown wrapping paper and the edges are smoothed with glue. (Brown paper is used because it won't tear when wet.)

22. The final layer of newsprint is then applied. Naturally, all the layers—especially the final ones—should be applied carefully to avoid unsightly creases and bulges. The edges of the final layer will, of course, show through the finished product.

PAPIER MÂCHÉ

235

FIGURE 6   FIGURE 7

23. Epaulets and braid, created out of strands of rope, are applied with glue. Immerse the cord in a bowl of Elmer's glue which is two parts glue to one part water. Remove the cord and squeeze out the excess glue so that the cord remains sticky. Apply to the soldier.

24. When all is dry, the figure is given two coats of white latex-base paint or gesso (Figure 7). Paint the cord also, but try not to let the gesso accumulate around it. Allow time for drying between the two coats.

25. Varnish is applied now to the areas that will be done in silver and gold leaf: the epaulets and braid. The varnish is applied with a narrow brush just as it comes from the container. Because the surfaces to be varnished are often small, a thin brush facilitates application *only* to the areas required. This must be done carefully.

26. Wait until the varnish becomes tacky (about 45 minutes), before applying the imitation silver and gold leaf. The leaf is applied with the fingers—no other tool is used (Figure 8). Press it on gently.

At the atelier the leaf is 16 by 16 *centímetros*, about $6\frac{1}{4}$ by $6\frac{1}{4}$ inches. If the leaf is too large, it is cut with scissors or torn with the fingers to a size just a little larger than the area to be covered. Once the leaf is applied to the varnish, remove the excess with your fingers or with a clean brush.

27. Now the figure is painted the desired colors with water-base paint (Figure 9). The facial details are done last. Take care not to get any paint on the gold or silver leaf.

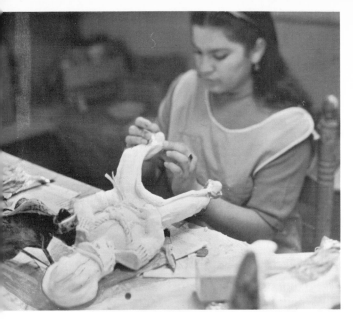

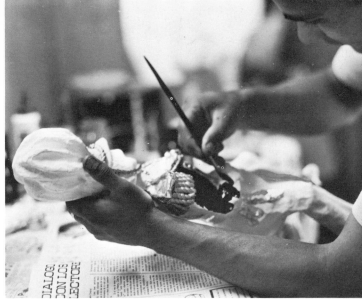

FIGURE 8   FIGURE 9

28. When thoroughly dry, the figure receives two coats of lacquer, either by spraying (Figure 10) or with a brush. By brush, the mixture is 2-parts lacquer to 1-part thinner. If you use the brush, use just enough lacquer so that it does not run or drip. *Do not rub the lacquer in.* Apply it lightly and smoothly.

Antiquing:

29. The antiquing is the most difficult part of the process. The entire figure, especially the crevices, is covered with a highly diluted water-base paint about the consistency of a cup of coffee, though some experimentation is advised. It is applied with a regular 3-inch brush.

At the *taller*, antiquing is done in various colors. The soldier was antiqued with black (Figure 11).

FIGURE 10

FIGURE 11

30. When it is dry, rub off the antiquing on the raised areas of the soldier with your fingers.

31. If you prefer less antiquing, dip a rag into the antique solution and squeeze out until the rag is damp. Then rub the surface with the damp rag.

You may use both methods. Fingers first, then the rag. However it is done, the antiquing brings out the texture of the papier-mâché and for the full beauty of the craft, the antiquing should not be omitted. If you are not satisfied with the result, simply dampen the rag, wipe off the antiquing, and try again.

32. Finally, the figure is given one more coat of lacquer. If the lacquer is brushed on, use 1-part lacquer to 1-part thinner. Be careful not to go over an area more than once. Again, it must be applied lightly and smoothly.

Allowing for the many drying times, the complete process takes about 10 days.

APPENDIXES

The Craftsmen

OJO DE DIOS and NEARIKA:
Padre Ernesto de Loera
Basilica de Zapopan
Zapopan, Jalisco
craftsmen: Teresa and Antonio
López Pineda

SERAPE:
Casimiro Amaro (son David)
Calle Sollano #42
San Miguel de Allende, Gto. (Guanajuato)

Lucha Mojica
C. Baeza #18
San Miguel de Allende
Guanajuato
craftsman: Fidel Méndez

PETATE:
Plácido Hernandez-Ramirez
c/o Casa de Sacerdote
Ihuatzio, Michoacán
(*Ihuatzio has no mail delivery. Mail is received through the priest.*)

CANASTO:
Agustín Pérez
c/o Casa de Sacerdote
Ihuatzio, Michoacán

CORAZÓN DE TRIGO:
Plácido Pablo
#247 Calle Convento
Tzintzuntzan, Michoacán
(and son, Plácido, Jr.)

FISH OF
SILVER:

Jesus Cazares
Obregon #52
Pátzcuaro, Michoacán

THE COPPER OF
SANTA CLARA:

José María Ruiz (Ruiz Hermanos)
Ocampo #222
Santa Clara del Cobre
Michoacán

TIN AND BRASS:

Eleuterio Llamas
Zacateros #9 (the shop.)
San Miguel de Allende
Guanajuato
(*Factory: Calle de Canal*)
craftsman: nephew, Javier Llamas.

THE BLACK
POTTERY OF
COYOTEPEC:

D. Rosa Real de Nieto
San Bartolo de Coyotepec
Oaxaca

TREE OF
LIFE:

Aurelio Flores
Benito Juarez #47
Izucar de Matamoros
Puebla

METEPEC SUN:

Timoteo González
Independencia #15
Metepec, Mexico

SANTO:

Domingo Galván
Av. Madero #307
Apaseo el Alto
Guanajuato
craftsman: Serafín Leon

THE LACQUER
OF URUAPAN:

Srta. Esperanza Hernandez
Calle del Caracol #33
Uruapan, Michoacán

THE MASKS
OF CELAYA:

Loreto Luna López
Ignacio López Barrera
Leandro Valle #627
Celaya, Guanajuato

Paulo Chico (wholesaler)
El Arte Celayenne
Madero #503
Celaya, Guanajuato

PAPIER-MÂCHÉ: Guy and Jeanne Schlee
Jeanne Valentine, S.A.
Pila Seca #28 (the factory)
San Miguel de Allende
Guanajuato
store: Calle Hidalgo in Hotel San Francisco

Table of Equivalents

Pesos:
100 centavos = 1 peso.
1 peso = 8 cents.
12.50 pesos = one dollar.

Liters:
1 liter = .26 gallons (a little over a quart).
1 gallon = about 3.8 liters.

Kilos (Kilograms):
1000 grams = 1 kilo.
1 kilo = approximately 2.2 pounds.
1 pound = approximately ½ kilo.

Temperatures:
Centigrade is 0° to 100°, freezing to boiling.
Fahrenheit is 32° to 212°, freezing to boiling.
(To convert Centigrade to Fahrenheit, multiply degrees by $\frac{9}{5}$ and add 32.
    To change Fahrenheit to Centigrade, subtract 32 first then multiply
    by $\frac{5}{9}$.)

Distances:
1 millimeter = about $\frac{3}{8}$ inch.
1 inch = about 2.5 centimeters.
10 millimeters = 1 centimeter.
100 centimeters = 1 meter.
1 meter = 39.37 inches, 3.28 feet, or 1.093 yards.
1 kilometer = .62 miles. (To approximate mileage, multiply by .6.)
100 kilometers = 62 miles.

Sources for Materials

The following is a list of sources of supply to aid the reader in finding necessary materials. It is not always possible to find in the United States all the materials used by the Mexican craftsman; he traditionally uses the materials close at hand.

Yarns and reeds seemed to be the most difficult to find. I have listed one reed supplier and several yarn suppliers who have been highly recommended. All will send catalogs and samples (most for a nominal fee of 50¢ to $1.00) upon request. One supplier, Greentree Ranch Wools, makes custom yarn.

Besides the yarn and reed suppliers, the reader may also contact:

> The American Crafts Council
> Research and Education Dept.
> 29 W. 53rd St., New York, New York 10019

for suppliers of various other materials, and:

School Arts Magazine which supplies a directory listing craft suppliers. Other possible sources to contact are the guilds of the various craftsmen here in the U.S., such as the basket weavers, the weavers, etc. (Many basket weavers, I am told, collect their own reeds by organizing trips to nearby swamps and marshes.)

For reeds: Cane and Basket Supply Co.
Dept C-12
1283 S. Cochran
Los Angeles, California
90019

For Yarn: Dharma Trading Company   (mailing address: P.O. Box 1288)
1952 University Ave.
Berkeley, California
94701

Folklorico
P.O. Box 625
Palo Alto, California
94302

Greentree Ranch Wools
Rt. 3, Box 461
Loveland, Colorado
80537

The Pendleton Shop
Jordan Road
Sedona, Arizona
86336

Someplace
2990 Adeline St.
Berkeley, California
94703

The Yarn Depot
545 Sutter St.
San Francisco, California
94102

Yarn Primitives
P.O. Box 1013
Weston, Connecticut
06880

These yarn companies either supply Mexican handspun yarns or their equivalents.

Bibliography

BOOKS

Appleton, Le Roy H. *Indian Art of the Americas.* New York: Charles Scribner's Sons, 1950.

Black, Mary E. *New Key to Weaving.* Milwaukee: The Bruce Publishing Company, 1968.

Burland, C. A. *The Gods of Mexico.* New York: G. P. Putnam's Sons, 1967.

Calderon de la Barca, *Madam Frances*, E. P. Dutton, 1946.

Cordry, Donald B., and Cordry, Dorothy M. *Mexican Indian Costumes.* Austin: University of Texas Press, 1968.

Covarrubias, Miguel. *Indian Art of Mexico and Central America.* New York: Alfred A. Knopf, Inc., 1957.

———, *Mexico South: The Isthmus of Tehuantepec.* New York: Alfred A. Knopf, Inc., 1964.

———. *The Eagle, the Jaguar, and the Serpent.* New York: Alfred A. Knopf, Inc., 1954.

Crow, John A. *Mexico Today.* New York: Harper & Row, Publishers, 1957.

Dockstader, Frederick J. *Indian Art in Middle America.* Greenwich, Conn.: New York Graphic Society Ltd., 1964.

Davis, Mary L., and Pack, Greta. *Mexican Jewelry.* Austin: University of Texas Press, 1963.

Diaz, del Castillo, Bernal. *The Discovery and Conquest of Mexico, 1517-1521.* New York: Farrar, Strauss and Giroux, 1956.

Dorner, Gerd. *Folk Art of Mexico.* A.S. Barnes & Co., Inc., 1962.

Faulkner, Herbert W. *Wood.* New York: Harper and Brothers, 1934.

Fernandez, Justino. *A Guide to Mexican Art.* Chicago: University of Chicago Press, 1961.

Girard, Alexander. *The Magic of a People.* New York: The Viking Press, Inc., 1968.

Gruening, Ernest H. *Mexico and Its Heritage.* Westport, Conn.: Greenwood Press, Inc., 1968.

Hoyt, Edith. *The Silver Madonna*. Mexico D.F.: Editorial Letras, S.A., 1963.

Hunt, W. Ben. *Contemporary Whittling and Carving*. Milwaukee: The Bruce Publishing Co., 1967.

Keleman, Pal. *Baroque and Rococo in Latin America*. Gloucester, Mass.: Peter Smith.

———. *Medieval American Art: Masterpieces of the New World Before Columbus*. New York: Dover Publications, Inc., 1969.

Museum of Modern Art and Instituto de Antropologia e Historia de Mexico. *Twenty Centuries of Mexican Art*. Mexico, 1940.

Nelson, Glenn C. *Ceramics—The Potter's Handbook*. New York: Holt, Rinehart & Winston, Inc., 1960.

Newton, Martha. *A Study of Mexican Handwoven Cloth from the Raw Material to the Finished Product*. [Thesis]. San Miguel de Allende, Mexico: Instituto Allende, 1960.

Nicholson, Irene. *The X in Mexico*. Garden City, N. Y.: Doubleday & Company, Inc., 1966.

Norman, James. *In Mexico*. New York: William Morrow & Co., 1959.

———. *Terry's Guide to Mexico*. Garden City, N. Y.: Doubleday & Company, Inc., 1972.

O'Gorman, Helen. *Plantas Y Flores De Mexico*. Mexico: Universidad Nacional Autonoma de Mexico, Direction General de Publicaciones, 1963.

Organismo de promocion internacional de cultura. *OPIC*. Mexico: Secretaria de Relaciones Exteriores.

Pack, Greta. *Jewelry Making for the Beginning Craftsman*. New York: D. V. Nostrand Company, Inc., 1957.

Paddock, John. *Ancient Oaxaca*. Stanford, Calif.: Stanford University Press, 1966.

Plan Chileno Mexicano de Cooperacion Fraternal Festividades de Noviembre 1964. *Arte Popular De Mexico*. Mexico, 1964.

Polhemus, Elbert D. *Teaching the Ancient Art of Serape Weaving to Contemporary Adults*. [Thesis]. San Miguel de Allende, Mexico: Instituto Allende, 1963.

Prescott, William H. *The Conquest of Mexico*. London: J. M. Dent & Sons, 1965.

Rhodes, Daniel. *Clay and Glazes for the Potter*. Philadelphia: Chilton Book Company, 1957.

Rioja Lo Bianco, Enrique; Ruiz Oronoz, Manuel; and Larios Rodriguez, Ignacio. *Tratado Elemental Zoologica*. Mexico D.F.: Editorial E.C.L.A.L.S.A., Libreria de Porrua Hnos, y Cia, S.A., 1966.

Rose, Augustus F., and Cirino, Antonio. *Jewelry Making and Design*. New York: Dover Publications, Inc., 1967.

Ross, Patricia F. *Made in Mexico: The Story of a Country's Arts and Crafts*. New York: Alfred A. Knopf, Inc., 1952.

Simon, Kate. *Mexico Places and Pleasures*. Garden City, N. Y.: Doubleday and Company, Inc., Dolpin Books, 1962.

Storm, Marion. *Enjoying Uruapan.* Mexico, 1945.

Toor, Frances. *A Treasury of Mexican Folkways.* New York: Crown Publishers, Inc., 1947.

———. *Mexican Popular Arts.* Mexico: Frances Toor Studio, 1939.

———. *New Guide to Mexico.* Revised by Kate Simon. New York: Crown Publishers, Inc., 1948.

Zechlin, Ruth. *The Complete Book of Handcrafts.* Newton Center, Mass.: Charles T. Branford Co., 1959-67

PERIODICALS

Boyd, E. "The New Mexico Santero." *El Palacio* (Quarterly Journal of the Museum of New Mexico), Spring 1969.

Canady, John. "Popular Art Versus Popular Dollars." *Mexican Life,* June 1969.

Cuellar, Elizabeth. "A Survey of Creative Metal Arts from the Prehispanic to the Modern." *Mexico This Month,* June 1969.

Eashy, Dudley T., Jr. "Early Metallurgy in the New World." *Scientific American,* April 1966.

Georgi, Audrey A. "Adventure in Glass." *Mexican Life,* August 1953.

Harvey, Marian. "Papier-Mâché-A La Mode." *American Artist,* February 1969.

Hastings, Morris C. "Pride of Oaxaca." *Mexican Life,* July 1954.

Holt, Rosemary Davis. "Veracruz Carnival." *Mexican Life,* April 1955.

Keleman, Pal. "The Weavers High Art." *Mexican Life,* January 1968.

Mexico This Month, "Carretones" 5, March-April 1969.

Peterson, Fred, A. "The Pottery of Ancient Mexico." *Mexican Life,* August 1952.

Ramirez, Alfonso Francisco. "Oaxaca Handicrafts." *Mexican Life,* July 1953.

Zendgui, Guillermo. "The Crisis in Folk Arts." *Mexican Life,* February 1970.

Agencies Mentioned

The Museo de Artes Populares, the Banco Fomento, and the Museo Antropológia are frequently mentioned in the book. These are the correct names:

The Museo Nacional de Antropológia, one of the world's finest and certainly its most beautiful archaeological museum, is found in Mexico City facing Paseo de la Reforma in Chapultepec Park. The second floor is dedicated to contemporary ethnic practices of the many Indian and mestizo groups within the country. Here the reader will find many crafts on display as well as realistic mock-ups of the procedures. The first floor is devoted to the rich pre-Conquest civilizations, their history and their art.

Museo Nacional de Artes y Industrias Populares, Juarez 44, across from the Alameda in Mexico City, maintains exhibition-salesrooms. The purpose of this museum is to preserve and improve the traditional crafts of Mexico by giving the craftsman an outlet for his work.

The Banco Fomento is the Banco Nacional de Fomento Cooperativo. Its exhibition-salesrooms are called the Salon de las Artesanías de Mexico. Both are located in the same building at the corner of Versalles and Atenas in Mexico City. A government operation, this is part of the National Bank of Cooperative Development. A trust fund has been set up to give credit to Mexican craftsmen as well as to preserve the design and techniques of their craft. This agency aids the craftsman in the marketing of his product, especially in finding new markets for him. They particularly concentrate on export.

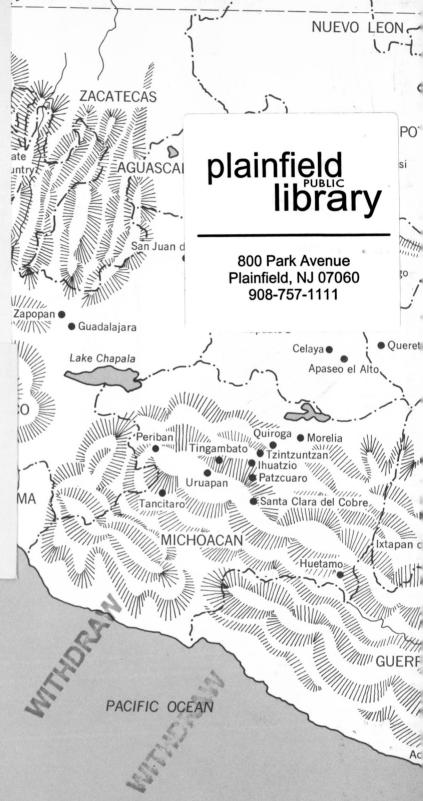

Scale

25   50 miles

THE BAJIO: THE HIGH VALLEY OF QUERETARO AND GUANAJUATO